THE TEAM
NOBODY
WOULD PLAY

THE TEAM NOBODY WOULD PLAY

BY

BUCK GODFREY

To Daniel —
I'm sure you're
familiar with the
Biblical Daniel.
Remain I ast as
faithful and
strong as you
young eyed show.
Always be
confident and
never fear!
Buck
Godfrey

DORRANCE PUBLISHING CO., INC.
PITTSBURGH, PENNSYLVANIA 15222

ISBN: 978-0-8059-7764-6
Library of Congress Control Number: 2007939474

Printed in the United States of America

First Printing

For more information or to order additional books, please contact:

Dorrance Publishing Co., Inc.
701 Smithfield Street
Third Floor
Pittsburgh, Pennsylvania 15222
U.S.A.
1-800-788-7654
www.dorrancebookstore.com

To C. Frank Yancey, the finest defensive coach to ever grace a sideline;

Eddie Robinson of Grambling, the greatest coach of all time;

Robbie Johnson, my high school football coach, who taught me how to win;

Joe Gilliam, Sr., Tennessee State's finest football mind;

Okella Mitchell, my mother-in-law, friend, and confidant;

Bailey Sky (Goyakla), my beautiful, energetic granddaughter;

and Joyce Elaine who accepted my flaws, gave me two fine children and kept my back even as she shared me with the world.

PREFACE

The *Team Nobody Would Play* is a vivid and touching docu-drama which, at the core, illustrates how the use of a bat, a ball and a glove galvanizes a community, challenges a racist system and ultimately vaults a select group of dedicated youngsters and coaches into American history. Set during the 1950's in Charleston, South Carolina, the work explores three main themes – innocence, the loss of innocence and the resulting development of the brooding man-child.

Written in the frame technique, the reader will laugh and amuse himself with the fun-loving, resourceful "traveling" team, the Kracke Court Sluggers, who never lost a game. Then the reader will venture into the world of the Charleston Little League All Stars who run the gamut of emotional highs and lows as they simply try to play baseball in a society which feared their skills and the very real threat of being the first to lose to an African-American team. Finally, in the chapter on Martin Park, where only the best play the best, the reader must decide how crippling – if at all – was the psychological, emotional, mental and social impact on these youngsters who were forever denied the right to compete for a championship in a place called America.

One of the players is the author, who is my father, William "Buck" Godfrey. Many an evening was spent in a poorly lit, hot, blue room typing, retyping, editing, re-editing, juggling and re-juggling chapter after chapter. No easy task this was, but we finished the course.

The work one reads is a culmination starting a few years ago at the Riverdog Stadium in Charleston. Most of the participants converged upon the city to be recognized for their slight and decided that this was a signature event in the history of our people which needed to be in book form. Ever the visionary, my father recorded those who were willing to talk. Some refused.

What he thought would be an easy task of transcribing conversation and writing a story turned into a monumental task. Key people in their eighties had not been interviewed, especially one coach, Mr. Rufus Dilligard. Also, Mrs. Bailey, a "walking encyclopedia" from the parents' side, had to be located and recorded. Consequently, many a trip, of which I was a part, took place from Decatur, Georgia, to Charleston. My father never faltered, and with proper networking with teammates John Bailey, Carl Johnson and Leroy Major, the story emerged.

Eloquently written, complete with dynamic poetry, the reader will receive an inside view of families and neighborhoods. He will experience a unique lifestyle and marvel at the endearing characteristics of a remarkable people. To add to its uniqueness, a touch of Gullah spoken by some of the players is present. One will visualize the shoddy fields of play, primitive transportation and pre-modern equipment. In spite of all, one will see a resilient, happy people and boys who loved the game of baseball.

I am proud to have been a part of this journey of work with my father to bring not closure, but real openness to this piece of history. Growing up, I've heard plenty of stories about my father and his friends from a lot of family members. Some of the stories were of Herculean proportions, but I never doubted them because of who he is, a very strong willed and powerful motivator, whose presence is immediately known. I only continue to pray and strive that my legacy will rival his in becoming a positive role model to my family and community. We are no doubt the best of friends and this journey together (interviews, riding from Decatur, Georgia, to Charleston, writing, typing) in the most extreme conditions in the summer of 2005, has made our bond that much more special. We are all proud of this story, and please enjoy your walk through a piece of unknown history.

—*Colin Josh Godfrey*

PROLOGUE

We grew up in a society that had silently, meticulously and sardonically crafted the blueprint for our ultimate failure. The process began early. African-American babies were delivered into the world at black Roper Hospital. When they arrived at a certain age, they were educated at supposedly inferior all black schools, thereby stunting their education. If they played with their white counterparts either at Bishop England or the Jewish Community Center and they became thirsty, an accommodating adult of the Caucasian race would usher them to a water fountain which had the term "colored" affixed to the top. Their white buddies, amazed by all of this, were directed to the fountain that read "whites only" at the top. If they continued in this relationship, the separation became habitual, and eventually they would resent each other without knowing why. This ignorance reached its maximum when it came to bathing in the great Atlantic Ocean. Since Charleston proper is a tributary, several beaches can be reached in less than fifteen miles. However, in order to bathe, a black family had to travel the seventy plus miles to Beaufort Beach, the eighty plus miles to McKenzie Beach or the 110 miles to Atlantic Beach. Sadly, all white Myrtle Beach was adjacent to Atlantic Beach, each parts of the great Atlantic.

To continue the process of psychological warfare, transportation was included. Blacks were required to sit at the back of the bus marked by a yellow line. To cross this line could place one in jail. This was the law. As for the media, The Charleston Evening Post and The News and Courier carried few stories of positive achievements by African Americans. If a positive article appeared, one needed a Sherlock Holmes type magnifying glass to read it. This vitriolic attack extended to the radio as well. The infamous "Amos 'n' Andy Show" now debuted. White voices in "black-face" blurted their version of the stereotypical ignorant, bumbling, henpecked black man, to the delight of both black and white ears. "But herein lies the rub" quotes Shakespeare. Blacks laughed because it was simply entertaining. To hear whites play the fool by voicing their impression of who they thought blacks were was hilarious. Tragically, whites laughed because they believed what they heard to be true and that increased their idea of superiority.

When television finally appeared, "Leave It to Beaver" became the prototype of order, virtue and the American way. The white Cleaver family was perfect; the father rattled off aphorism after aphorism while his doting wife, always nattily dressed for a tea party, marveled at his wisdom. The boys were unbelievably disciplined, mild-mannered and as unreal as Superman. Nevertheless, this was the media's ideal of a perfect family and some people probably believed this.

Finally, there was the ultimate insult to the African-American man, the caricature in marble or china of the Black Sambo. Many appeared on well manicured lawns around Charleston and the surrounding areas. Fresh off the plantation, Sambo was the ever-loyal, smiling, docile "darkie" whom whites loved because he was asexual and harmless. Always shiny, dark and dressed in red, his presence meant that the owner of the house saw blacks as so many children who, when behaving poorly, were simply a nuisance that had to be whipped or lynched.

Oddly enough, all of this had just a minimal negative effect on the African-American. What the system and its perpetrators did not factor into the equation was this. During segregation, black men and women were more cognizant of family, love, survival and education. Strong families made for strong neighborhoods and strong neighborhoods established strong ties to history and culture. A natural phenomenon followed. Blacks already knew the white man and his ways, but the relationship he had with him changed from fear and evasion to indifference and polarity, primarily because of oral reinforcement from the elderly and veterans returning from overseas.

The elderly, held in the highest esteem by the black community, communicated wisdom in a colorful and positive way largely through anecdotes and testimonies. Service men added a deeper flavor, sweetened or soured by experience abroad. To this knowledge of the elders, they gave affirmation by exposing the world as it was and is. Their overseas experience had made them vocal and manly, and the community responded.

Consequently, the William Lynch School of fear and intimidation suffered foreclosure long before the brutal death of Emmitt Till. Richard Wright's sullen, angry and ignorant character, Bigger Thomas, would fear no more. He had found a caring father and mother who would show him why he felt like he did, and give direction. Naturally, they made sure he attended school regularly, and they would "crack the whip" if need be. In a like manner, Claude Brown's "manchild" was just as brazen, but he did not have to fight his societal battles totally by himself because he now had a father who was privy to the ways of the enemy. As a result, Claude had a trusted and willing ally. Finally, "pre-individualism" as a safety net was not practiced until needed. Individual achievement, especially in academics, was praised. However, if the individual became threatened by the enemy because of "unacceptable" behavior, then the family, the neighborhood, and the community came to his aid and they protected him. One of the most important and least mentioned aspects, which was truly an asset and source of pride during this time, was the presence of our <u>necessaries</u>. The teacher made doubly sure that one learned. The lessons presented incorporated the background and experience of the student so interest levels soared and high achievement was the result. As a plus, the teacher usually lived in or near one's neighborhood and if a student showed enough interest and tact, he could possibly be helped on weekends. On Cannon and Spring Streets, one could find black dentists, doctors and lawyers. I still sport the beautiful results of dental work performed by Dr. Pickering and Dr. Caffey some forty-four years ago. The important thing here is their children were our playmates and attended the same schools as we did. This enhanced socialization and eliminated class structure or status.

The real source of pride was the flourishing of African-American businesses during segregation. Henry Smith and Bubba Middleton owned service stations and made big money. Mr. Taylor's bakery shop on Spring Street near King was famous for his butterfly buns and cinnamon rolls. Many a Saturday, we smuggled these goodies into either the Lincoln or Palace – the black theaters on King Street. When a fellow went swimming in the pool behind Harmon Field, his hunger usually drove him to enjoy one of Scotty's "greasy-good" link bologna sausages that popped when bitten. Scotty's Soda Shop was located right across from Harmon Field on President Street and Fishburn. Finally, Mr. Whitney and Mr. Foster owned convenience stores – the former at the corner of Ashley Avenue and Line Street; the latter, "Back the Green" and Mr. Brooks, the proprietor of Brooks Restaurant and Lounge on Morris Street, touted the best lima bean dinner in America.

Lastly, the black community had a unique way of communicating or receiving news: the party lines, across the backs of fences, pokeno parties, gossip, the church, joking at the work place, or the corner. King's barbershop on Line Street was another. Most of the men in the shop had already read and digested important items concerning our people from The Pittsburgh Courier, The Baltimore Afro-American or The Norfolk Journal and Guide. Jet and Ebony were also perused for information. Some, who would later dominate the conversation, had called a relative in New York City to see what the Brooklyn Dodgers had done the previous night. Soon talk came fast and furious. Arguments ended with a belly laugh. Topics included who died smiling and who died frowning, then the Negro League and the Big League, followed by women, religion, and politics, then Larry Doby, Hank Aaron, Willie Mays and on and on and on. That's how we received real news.

As one can discern, these ploys by people who would destroy us never really developed. In fact, segregation provided a positive isolation wherein we Africans maintained our culture, our language and our religion. Because of our strong family ties, upstanding neighborhoods and powerful communities, we never became victims of fear or non aggression. The psychological and social interaction with our peers and their competitive spirit toughened us and made us stout and strong – black Charleston style. Big brothers like Herbie Nelson, Chunk, Tommy Rue, Feaster, Fat Boy, Pepsi, Teddy Wright, Sammy Heart, Tub, Ike, Stuffy Jefferson and Chicken kept us in line. They all wanted us to do well. No matter the circumstances there would be a solution. We were the fruit of a fertile harvest and we had a mission responsibility to represent our people and our culture to their fullest degree.

Our story begins in a variety of black neighborhoods in Charleston, South Carolina, in the middle and late 1950's. It meanders to the shores of the Susquehanna River in Williamsport, Pennsylvania, and then diffuses to points north – New York City, suburban New Jersey and Washington, D.C. As in any literary endeavor, there are heroes and villains, good and evil, fact and fiction – in fine, a story with a beginning, middle, and an end. Nevertheless, this work is special because it is a part of American history – real, vibrant, powerful – as strong as my father's fresh-brewed blend of Luzianne and Maxwell House coffees. The protagonists are the coaches at Harmon Field and Martin Park and fourteen twelve-year-olds who played the game of baseball so flawlessly and effortlessly that their legacy has become the stuff of legend in Charleston sports folklore. Another special aspect of the work follows and is indicative for a more intimate, more profound and more meaningful understanding of the story.

Throughout the course of the narrative, original commentaries by the players and coaches appear. Their purpose is to illustrate, to emphasize and to clarify certain points of interests. Recorded in an informal setting at the Riverdog Stadium, an interesting phenomenon presents itself. Although these men have traveled to and lived in various geographic areas, vestiges of Gullah, the language of the black man in the South Carolina low country and Sea Islands, still remain in their speech patterns. Basically, Gullah illustrates the dynamic coalescence of Africanisms and Pidgin English. It is exciting to know that as native Charlestonians, they have maintained this uniqueness of morphology and phonology which add to the color and originality of their language and, of course, their story.

Many examples of Gullah abound. One will discover that the letter "d" or "t" replaces the soft eth (ð) sound in such words as dat (that), wid (with) or wit (with). There is also the use of the schwa (ə) (pronounced here as ah or uh) to replace the letter "a" or "I" in such expressions as um for I'm and ləv for live. Also, clipping occurs at the beginning and end of words. Accordingly, across becomes 'cross. About becomes 'bout. Talking emerges as talkin'. Him becomes 'im.

The use of double negative for emphasis is also unique; *"Ain't nobody gon' hit 'im"* or *"a dead man don'(t) do no harm 'cause he can't."* Problematic for the casual reader could be the use of verb tense. The invariant "be" covers all tenses. I be sick today; I be sick tomorrow; I be sick yesterday–present, future, past. Furthermore, the use of verb tense is determined by the time sequence of the action or person described. It is seen as continuing action begun in the past and evolving in the present.

My teammate, Leroy Major's "hustle" account will help to clarify some of these points, especially the use of verb tense. *"We grew up, I sell rag, iron, moonshine bottles–a case for sixty cents and we hustled. We use to go down to the grocery stores and when the people come out–mostly black people because they didn' have vehicles and stuff so we had our little wagons (that) we made. And take and say, 'Call that lady right dey', then when the person come out, we say, 'Ma'am, can I take your groceries home for you?' And she said, 'Yes!' We roll the grocery home, get a dollar (as a tip, come back to the grocery store). An' that's how we would (hustle)."*

One will also note in Leroy's portrayal that the use of pronouns is interchangeable from singular to plural. In a group effort, the I (singular individual) is functionally effective only as it serves to enhance the importance of the <u>we</u> pronoun. The <u>we</u> encompasses the combined effort of the group of individuals in search of a common goal – always of utmost importance to the speakers of Gullah. In effect, the success of the group is always more important than the success of the individual.

The use of incomplete sentences is also used by the speaker of Gullah. For the most part, these are verbalized thought patterns that emerge randomly and are normally indicative of a sense of urgency. Another of my teammates, Arthur Peoples, wants to play ball. Nothing will stand in his way. *"Come from school. Run home. Get our homework, back to the park."* There is no apology for his urgency. In essence, he simply means that this is important to me. Forget the rules of standard American grammar. Make sense of what I said, and meet me at the park. Essentially, our culture is different and our speech is different, but here we are. Unknowingly, we are challenging the sincerity of your interest. Do you have a good enough ear to hear me? Believe what I say because it is important to me. It is the way I feel, and I want you to understand, but you must stay with me because I'm moving fast.

As such, it is hoped that this brief introduction into our way of living and speaking will enhance one's enjoyment. If the reader can understand that not only was our team unique, our parents and coaches unique, our culture unique and our "language" unique, especially when the speaker is emotionally charged, he can better enjoy us Gullah-speaking Geechies who played and coached baseball so well that we became known as *The Team Nobody Would Play.*

CHAPTER I

In the dewy, pristine world
Of early morning secrets,
Lavender morning glory flowers
Would open mysteriously, elegantly
To the bluebird and cardinal.
In the evening, the red and white
Of the four o'clock
Would repeat the process
To the swallow and bull bat.
Chores would be done
In an orderly fashion.
The yard would be swept clean,
Smooth as black velvet,
With no grass to be seen.
During the week,
Beans and butts,
Steamed and fried,
Covered plates or pans of rice.
A light breeze would blow
Filling the air with the sweet smell
Of honeysuckle and pee the bed-
Another lazy, pleasant day.
On Friday, the smell of red rice
And fish saturated the air.
This was a savory ritual.
A drunk or two muttering to themselves would meander
Through the block
And disappear

In one of the various "cracks"
Where there was another drink
Of King Kong and Scrap Iron at the ready.
The Saturday night bath
Either by foot tub
Or by bathtub-
Hot water toted and poured.
Daddy first, then Mama,
Then the children,
The brown soap enduring it all.
Each neighborhood, mine or yours.

"I was born on 18 Duncan Street. Saw a little bit of segregation. I grew up in a poor neighborhood, but I didn't know I was poor because everyone would give each one what they needed. If you needed grits and you didn't have any, you'd take your cup next door and get a cup of grits.

"Everyone used to come to my mother's house on Saturday (morning) for pancakes. So all the kids would have pancakes on Saturday (morning). Kids used to call my mother Aunt Vi, and some of the kids still think I'm their cousin. We didn't need a babysitter because all the older kids would baby-sit the smaller ones. We never locked our door (at night) except for once a year when we went out of town. Otherwise, the doors were always unlocked when we went to bed at night because everybody in the neighborhood looked out for each other and we all act(ed) like family."

—Leroy Major

"I was raised in Strawberry Lane–a neighborhood known for cuttin', shootin' and fighting. There was so much hell raising that the four of us–myself, my two brothers and sister–could never play half rubber outside of the six-foot chain link fence which surrounded our yard unless we were supervised. On most days we would just wait for my daddy to come home from work and take us to Harmon Field. Otherwise, things were pretty good.

"Mr. Dave, my neighbor who fathered thirteen children, would have oyster roasts and crab boils, where good-doing people would gather and listen to tales of the Negro League. My mother, Miss Flossie, would always have her pots of *collard greens, ham hocks, rice, potato salad and fried chicken for needy families. So there was some stability and love in my neighborhood."*

—John Bailey

"I lived in a place called Islincoln Court. It was a perfect example of how a segregated society defined neighborhoods just by the irony of white and black families living next door to each other, but never socializing. Some black children and white children played together. But some white adults wouldn't allow this.

"I remember that in my neighborhood, there was a white boy named Sonny. His parents would not allow him to play with us. He would watch us through his fence as we played sandlot baseball. I could tell he was dying inside. (The sad part) is he had no idea of a segregated society. (But the adults would eventually get to him)."

—John Rivers

"I grew up in Gadsen Green Projects known as "Back the Green". In my family, there are thirteen of us–seven boys and six girls. Segregation was very strong in those days, so being raised in the projects was tough. We could not go various places to enjoy ourselves, such as restaurants, beaches and a lot of other places. So we stayed close in the project.

"We played a lot of ball–basketball, football, and baseball, (but) the main thing we did was enjoy each other. We were respectful to our parents and the parents of our friends. It took a village to raise a child, and back then, everybody was your parent. If a grownup see you doing wrong, you get a spanking right then and there. And when you got home, you'll get another one. That's the way it was then."

—Vermont Brown

"When you live here (Charleston), it was a little tough comin' from one side of town to the other. Where I was from on Morris Street, it was like a war zone.

All the area was pretty bad. I had to fight my way to practice on Harmon Field where I didn't know anybody. But in and around Morris Street, we had some tough guys.

"Rouse, John John, Kinsey, Bill Cody and a(n) older fellow John Nolan who like to shoot guns. All of them loved to fight, as I had to duck and dodge just to leave home. Every so often one would catch you and either slap you up side the head or kick you in the pants. It was rough. Then I had to go back home after practice or a game, and try to duck these same fellows. But I managed."

—Carl Johnson

We came from different neighborhoods, but our parents knew each other either from church membership, work place or social gatherings. We knew the existence of segregation, but not the vicious brutality of it. Our parents had insulated us from its sting. For the most part, we were all poor; however, we never knew it. Our parents saw to that also. We all loved baseball and our parents enjoyed watching us play. And we could play well. We were the 1955 Charleston, South Carolina, Little League All Stars.

Everybody who was anybody in Charleston played baseball. It was The Game. The favorite team was the Brooklyn Dodgers largely because of the presence of Jackie Robinson, Roy Campanella, Don Newcombe, Joe Black, and Junior Gilliam. Of course, there were other great players whom we emulated and some of us copied their styles. Many youngsters like me, who could run, catch and hit, wanted to be Willie Mays, Hank Aaron, Ernie Banks or Frank Robinson. We would imitate Willie Mays' famous "basket catch", field grounders like the smooth Ernie Banks and hit like Frank Robinson and Hank Aaron–level cut with quick wrists and a keen eye. All of us had a special broomstick or tree limb on which we would cut the players' name into the wood along with his jersey number and batting average. These we would varnish and pine tar. Later, we would put a notch near the handle end for every homerun we hit. We would dream of playing in the Big League, but for the moment there was the happiness and sanctity of our neighborhoods. It was there that we learned the game.

Some of us lived on dirt streets called courts. There was Kracke Court, Kennedy Court, Islincoln Court and Rosemont Court. Living on a dirt street had advantages. It was not only a playground and a natural baseball field, but also a wrestling mat and football field. Some of the hardest hitting in the world would occur on crisp, winter weekends. Others lived on paved streets like America Street, Judith Street, Line Street, Bogard Street and Morris Street. Others cut their baseball teeth in Gadsen Green Projects where there was both grass and dirt, but too many clotheslines for any real space. Nevertheless, given a rubber ball, a good broomstick or three and some free time, a game of baseball would happen.

"We didn't have bats or league balls so we used mop sticks or broom sticks. Our balls were tennis balls cut in half and our gloves were a paper bag or cut down cardboard box. We played until nighttime and get up the next day and repeat it. This was our life."

—Vermont Brown

Neighbors played and it transcended age and gender. On Kracke Court, "Light Bee", a full grown woman, could hit the daylights out of a ball. She could also run and field with the best of the men. Since the base paths were straight–about sixty yards from home to first—meant that Ruthie Mae Singleton could play. She was lightning fast and could hit. Thellie (I never learned her real name) might have been the best football/baseball player on anyone's team. Everyone wanted her on their team. The balls would fly. Some would go into the abandoned lot where all the weeds were; others would hit the roof on Dart Hall Library and skip to the brier-filled yard at its rear; but people would have fun and never a "rough" word was spoken or yelled. Games ended for one of three reasons: loss of balls, darkness or just plain fatigue. Somehow the score did not matter much. People just enjoyed each other and had a good time.

Needless to say, a rubber ball was sacred. It was at various times the reason for getting out of bed, hating an unexpected rainstorm or going to bed feeling high or low. Also, the dime that we used to purchase a ball came with a price. Some of us would sell Coke bottles or copper wire to earn it. Others of us would catch and sell blue crabs which we caught in a "forbidden" creek behind the Citadel. The crabs would sell quickly at fifty cents a dozen but the work involved in catching them was rough. This last endeavor made the ball even more precious.

To catch crabs required organization. We needed chicken backs and necks for bait; we needed soda crackers and sardines for food; we needed to go shopping. And shop we did. "Scutta", the Greek who owned the store at the corner of Bogard and Ashley, would give my brother Frank our midday rations. He was nice and never "charged" us by asking for crabs. He had the balls we purchased so I suppose he figured that our business relationship balanced. But he took care of us. He was nice like that. Then after his son graduated from the Citadel, he left, just like that.

The butcher at Rodenberg's wasn't so nice. When he saw us approaching, he would pack a bunch of half–rotten chicken backs and necks in a croacker sack, then throw it near our feet. Although he was a big man with a meat cleaver, it took a lot of restraint for Doug and I not to kick his ass. If we didn't need the bait, we probably would have tried. He grinned at us through his tobacco stained teeth and put up ten clumsy fingers. We would give him his ten blue crabs that afternoon. But make no mistake about it, we had plans for him come Halloween. Cord we had from kite season. Our homemade dip net with the chicken wire attachment was ready.

The next morning at 6:00, we packed our "works" and placed them in the red "Radio-Flyer" wagon. Anything else we threw over strong backs. The tide was right. The west wind was right. All that was left now was negotiating the trip to the creek. Some referred to this trip as the Underground Railroad. The world which we were about to enter was not too far removed from that of Harriet Tubman. Older blacks avoided this area. Somehow it didn't faze us. I guess we hadn't learned to fear. We were crazy like that.

This distance covered two miles. We left Kracke Court, crossed President, walked by Johnson–Hagood Stadium and entered Hagood Avenue. We were in the land of refuge constructed by whites to defend themselves against another Denmark Vesey. We passed General Mark Clark's house and came face to face with the deep South in the guise of the Citadel.

The guards, clad in their somber gray uniforms, seemed not to notice us. They were more interested in the comings and goings of the steady stream of cars filled with visitors. Passing through the pedestrian gate, we moved to the square, a football field rectangle surrounded by foreboding gray buildings and walkways. Tourists peered intently at the silent cannons, forever sealed by cement, and inoperable planes now grounded in defeat. These people seemed, by their resigned demeanor, to reflect on a time long ago that defined their being in the present. So sad. A couple of khaki–clad security personnel, without the energy to speak, gave us a dull look of disdain as we nonchalantly continued on our way. We soon saw our destination. Excitedly, we ran pass the Mess Hall, across the railroad track to the bridge. There was the creek.

With the fine-tuned skill honed by experience, we set out lines for the incoming tide. The crabs started in almost immediately. With methodical ease, we slowly pulled the lines to the trusty wire net. At times, two or more crabs would take one bait. Within an hour, we had caught at least sixty. We caught a few more big ones just before high tide. Since the crabs didn't bite well then, this was our time to eat and swim.

After gobbling down a bit of sardines and soda crackers and chasing it with sweet water from mason jars, we stripped and hit the water. It was cool and salty. This was our reward and we enjoyed it. While treading vigorously, we splashed water into each other's face, played a game called "shark", then climbed the still sturdy boards of the bridge to swan dive. After four or five "Tarzans", we ended one phase of our water venture, and entered another. Challenging ourselves, we swam to the mouth of the creek where the current was strongest as it entered the Ashley River. The pull was powerful like we were. However, knowing the danger, we never lingered long before swimming against the current to the safety of the bridge. Just five little black boys with not a care in the world, enjoying the cool water of the inlet.

Ebb tide came. This meant the creek water was moving back to the river and crabbing would be good again. Clothes on, lines out, lines in, net out, crabs in the bucket. This continued until we had our share, around twelve dozen. At two o'clock, we packed up the "works" with the crabs and started back as we had come. There was no incident. It's always better to travel the Underground Railroad in the daytime. We weren't that crazy. Ah! Kracke Court.

We would now sell the crabs and we took care of our regular customers first: Miss Hattie, Mr. Jimmy, Light Bee, Big Maybelle and Miss Pearl. We never made it to Spring Street from Kracke Court before all of our crabs were sold except ten. Now we had spending money. We had ball money. But, after all that effort, we had "predators".

In my neighborhood, we had four that could put the life of a ball in jeopardy. Of course, there were the long, towering blasts that oftentimes crossed Bogard Street and landed in any one of several backyards. At least sixteen eyes traced the arc followed by eight pairs of PF Flyers. More often than not, we retrieved it, but some were lost. Then there were drains or manhole covers along the sidewalks of Charleston. Each had about a three feet by eight inch rectangular opening to catch flood water. But they also inhaled our wayward rolling treasures. These we could not retrieve.

Next, there was Miss Nellie, a cross-eyed buxom woman about six feet tall and bowlegged. She had a sour meanness about her and the temperament to make it work. She also had the evil eye and could put the "mouth" on you. After hearing her fill of "ball noise", she would lean on her porch railing, beaming fire and brimstone. If a ball found its way to her yard, she would blurt out these words which later became synonymous with pain: *"Okay: Ya'll res' ya nerve!"* And she never returned any ball. Not even the bravest or quickest of us would challenge Miss Nellie. She had the evil eye.

Finally, there was Miss Butler, an old maid and the lady who ran Dart Hall Library at the corner of Bogard and Kracke. Now she was beyond mean and would even call the police if she felt we were making too much of a racket. Her backyard was small, and the room adjoining it served as a kitchen/dining area. In other words, she could see you enter her backyard if she were eating. Anyway, around the backyard she built a twelve foot green fence, sprinkled at the top with barbed wire. She also bought a watchdog, a boxer. But the real threat was her sister, the widow Dart, whom all of us believed to be a ghost. Her face was the color of a catfish's belly, long and drawn, with a shock of white hair that protruded to her eyebrows. In her slit of a mouth were two long, yellow canine teeth. And she always dressed in a long flowing hooded gown – either pure white or funeral black.

If the ball fell in Miss Butler's yard, all of us fell silent. Fear gripped us. We had to pull straws. This was automatic. If a guy pulled short, this was the procedure. One of us would take a tin of black pepper, which we kept for this moment, run to the front of the yard and sprinkle it through the chain link fence into the grass. The boxer would come growling and snarling at the "intruder". Then he would sniff that pepper. Sneezing and red-eyed, he would forget his duty. Two other guys would boost "short straw" up the fence. Now he would have to locate the ball, negotiate the barbed wire, jump into the yard, escaping all the fears of Miss Butler, the widow and the distracted boxer, grab the ball, throw it over the fence and finally, scale back over. This was not as hard as one might perceive–it took all of two minutes. But most of the time, if the ball went over the big, green fence, the bravest of us turned timid, and we knew we would rather find bottles or copper to sell, or plan a crabbing trip.

About the age of ten or so, we were hitting a rubber ball so accurately and consistently that we had to find a challenge. Mentally, we started preparing ourselves for something more difficult. I know hardball was on the horizon, but we were a year away. One evening, my father stopped the Dodge and talked to us about half rubber with the same earnestness in his voice that he used when he talked about Joe Louis or Sugar Ray Robinson, his favorite fighters. He concluded with this. *"If you can hit a half ball with a broomstick, then you'll find out if you jus' a batter or a hitter."* And he drove off to his second job.

With a pocket knife, we carefully cut a rubber ball in half. It looked strange and felt strange especially when we tried to pitch it. After experimenting with several grips, we decided on the index, thumb and middle fingers as the best way to pitch it. The fun and frustration started as that little flying saucer curved, dropped, rose and "butterflied" by our swinging sticks. This was the first time that the batter would actually rather pitch because it became embarrassing. Imagine trying to hit a drunken lightning bug in the dark with the cue end of a black pool stick. That was how difficult it was to hit half a ball that, when thrown, defied all laws of gravity and physics.

But persistence paid off. After a while, most of the fellows in our crowd could hit a half rubber. The process was simple. Pick up the ball when the pitcher's arm came through. Then watch the ball on the broomstick. Unknowingly, we were developing hand-eye coordination and an inside/out swing. This became an invaluable asset in the future when some of us would face great pitching.

Soon, what was later to be defining reality for future players of the Little League at Harmon Field and the East Side and the Pony League at Martin Park started to emerge. Interest started with the arrival of a regulation baseball-sized rubber ball. Shortly thereafter, hard ball emerged. Through a natural process of love for the game, neighborhoods began to have loosely organized teams. Now we needed more space because we would need four bases and an outfield. Plus, we would need regulation wooden bats and cowhide balls. But we did not have the money. For one more summer we played straight bases, but with the larger rubber ball, two gloves–one for the first basemen and one for the catcher who also had a mask–all of which we hustled. Our bats were tree limbs, straight smooth and grip worthy–all made possible with our knowledge of using a pocket knife. And we had fun, mainly because we were always winning. As I recall, the last game we played using a rubber ball was in Kennedy Court. Never were so many hits produced by so little: Kracke Court Sluggers 17, Kennedy Court 3.

As far as I know, we were the only team that had a name, at least on the Westside. Some of us were getting a little stout and a little cocky. We needed to play hardball and we were in need of everything. No problem. The last vestiges of the Negro League would play games on Sunday at College Park.

We were there, not as spectators, but as foul ball hustlers. And with eleven of us, we got our share.

To get bats, gloves and catching equipment, we went on the beg. After the game, Rip (Douglas Ashley) and I saw a tall, wiry gentleman in his sixties placing bats, balls, gloves, everything into about five or six duffle bags. Our first intention was to put on the *"Oh, mister, please!"* routine. Instead, we just walked up to him and told him our situation. Either he was caught off guard, or he saw himself in us, or God's grace just filled the dugout, but he gave us one of those duffle bags. We were elated and must have thanked him fifty times. He just winked at us and said, *"Go have some fun!"* We never got his name but it must have been Michael or Gabriel. In that bag was our legacy–two broken thirty-four ouncers and two sturdy thirty-six ouncers–all Louisville Sluggers. A breast protector, a pair of shin guards and an old face mask plus three new balls completed the contents of the bag. Later that evening, we took small nails, some sand-paper and a roll of athletic tape to repair the broken bats. We were set.

Each neighborhood had a team and we would play against each other. Our team, the Kracke Court Sluggers, would play anybody, any time, any place and we never lost a game. Our biggest challenge came when we played a team from Morris Street on a garbage strewn, weedy field behind the Cannon Street Y.M.C.A. Another concern faced us. All our opponents prior to this were our age–eleven and twelve, but the Morris Street team had older guys–fifteen, seventeen and we could swear, some twenty-year-olds. A final problem was the area.

As Carlie Johnson said, there were some bad dudes that lived around here—Rouse, John John, Kinsey, Frank, and the baddest of all, Bill Cody. All could and would fight or start something that none of us wanted because it meant defending our manhood, but we played. Alvin "Coffee" Thompson threw a three hitter; we played flawless defense and Hamp, Fat Boy and I struck for long homeruns. We blanked them and felt pretty good about it. Surprisingly, they were good sports. Even Rouse and Kinsey shook our hands and they did not even play. John John and Bill Cody remained aloof, which was fine with us. We knew then we had arrived. We were legit. All we wanted to do was leave the area without incident. This accomplished, Islincoln Court, Strawberry Lane, the East Side and teams from Grant Hill and Congress Street met the same fate.

On Saturdays, eleven of us would load Michael's/Gabriel's equipment on bikes and pedal the twelve or so miles to a field near Gresham Meggett High School on James Island. Upon arriving, we would all drink mighty gulps of the fresh water that came from a pump near the field. Refreshed and hydrated, we were ready to play.

The diamond was actually the smoothest part of a scraped down cornfield. Naturally, there was no fence so the scores would sometimes be double digits. When we competed on James Island, we played for money. Each player from each team would put up a pot of a dollar a man, which the umpire kept. At the end of the first game, each of us would receive a dollar and leave the dollar we had won with the umpire as payment for the second game.

After the second nine innings, we would collect our money, tip the umpire and load our equipment on our bikes, Next, we would drink our fill of the fresh well-water and hump back to Charleston proper by way of Folly Road and the Ashley River Bridge. Later, in our respective homes, a little tired, but real satisfied, we washed off, ate a butter or jam sandwich and slipped into a heavy sleep.

CHAPTER II

Whenever a man asks me
'What to do?'
Or when another man
Asks an opinion about doing
Anything,
I walk away
Because he is a fool
With his mind already made up.
But Mr. Mitchell was a gentleman,
The most humble of men.
His humility was never conceived
As meek or weak or phony.
He was simply a man,
Who knew what to do
And did it.

"The Charleston Little League All Stars [was] the result of the work of a community. Except for traveling teams like the Sluggers–and this was dangerous what they did–little black boys had nothing to do. The white boys had everything they wanted. The little black boys had nothing. To help alleviate this situation many people began to move in the direction of organization.

"Foremost were paying members of the Charleston Bears, originally the Blue Devils. We were a semi-pro football team who played in the park on Calhoun Street in the borough. Eventually, the Bears ran the Boys Club on Mary

Street at the old Mary Street School. The first idea of Little League came from our members while we operated the Boys Club. Remember, the Boys Club along with the Longshoremen started the East Side Little League in 1956.

"Prior to this, establishing a club at Harmon Field came up in our talks. As far as I can remember, the members of the Bears who began this endeavor were Lee Bennett, Fred Ballard, Paris Jenkins, Joe Scott, Anderson Whaley, Willie Wragg and George Lucas. All these were paying members. These were the original Little League pioneers.

"We needed a charter so Allen Tibbs, the Executive Secretary of the Y.M.C.A., added his expertise with paperwork. The white folks did not want us to be organized with a charter. In fact, they went out their way to postpone it and block it. In the end, I believe he dealt strictly with the national people in Williamsport. That's how the Y.M.C.A. got involved–and, because of Mr. Tibbs, the Cannon Street version which had moved from Coming Street.

"The Y.M.C.A. sent out word that adults were needed to volunteer as coaches and helpers for a Little League at Harmon Field. This was 1954. Lee Bennett and Fred Ballard whipped everybody with Pan Hellenic, but in 1955, we were gonna go national."

—Rufus Dilligard, Coach

The news hit with a bump. Small talk in the barbershops and on street corners gave way to a mission statement and challenge in the neighborhoods. The Cannon Street Y.M.C.A. had started organized baseball for boys aged ten through twelve. There would be coaches and uniforms and real Little League equipment. There would be real bases and a fence for homeruns. Games would be played at Harmon Field about a mile from any place in Charleston, so it seemed. All a player needed was a birth certificate, a baseball glove and cleats, and parental permission. What started as a subdued whisper now became a loud roar. The news had bumpety bumped into an avalanche of frenzied activity.

Boys who had stayed on the porch started to find a little manhood by asking their parents to buy them a glove and a bat. They would try out. Gyp and other hustlers would be scouting in order to "pad" their bets in the future. Good-hearted mothers and fathers led by Mrs. Bailey, Mrs. Major, Mrs. Dilligard and Mr. Jackson were organizing fund raisers. Most of all, a bunch of boys who never had any type of organization would finally be placed in a position to harness their talent, hone it and put it on display. This was our chance, our shot to be Willie Mays and Hank Aaron and Ernie Banks and Roy Campanella–oh boy! Tryouts began.

Imagine eight coaches in charge of working out 100 plus boys who were all trying to fill sixty slots. There were four teams: Harleston Funeral Home, Pan Hellenic Council, Police Athletic League and Fielding Funeral Home and each would take fifteen players. The coaches were Mr. Dilligard and Mr. Bennett, Pan Hellenic; Mr. Burke, P.A.L.; Mr. Singleton, Fielding; and Mr. Graham, Harleston. Certain guys wanted to play for certain coaches. Other guys wanted to play for a team with uniforms of a certain color: the navy blue and gray of P.A.L.; the green and gray of Fielding; the royal blue and gray of Pan Hellenic; or the red and gray of Harleston. The bottom line was that there were sixty slots only. Talent would be one of the deciding factors. And in the end, the real players did not care about who they played for or the color of the uniform. They just wanted to play.

The competition was fierce. Outfielders were separated from infielders. Potential pitchers and catchers were given special looks. Just about every part of Harmon Field was dotted with sweating little boys giving everything they had. Clearly, experience and savvy would be the ticket to play organized ball.

Outfielders shagged fly balls and fielded grounders. There were throws to second, third and home. The pressure of these drills was magnified by the presence of family, friends and peers. A player felt the need to be "perfect" as he left a line of perhaps twenty-five or thirty of his competitors to catch fly balls to his left, to his right, in the gap and, most difficult, right at him. This accomplished, he had to make a "perfect" throw to second, then third, then home. After three days of workouts, the field had narrowed and a pecking order was established. John Bailey, Allen Jackson, Charles Bradley, Leroy Major and myself were big timers.

The same grueling drills were accorded the infielders: hard grounders, one hop shots, top spin and cut spin were directed at them. "Perfect" again entered the picture. "Perfect" throws to first, to second, to home. Situation drills with the coach yelling: *"Man on second and third–no outs, one out, two outs."* Field, think, throw! Field, think, throw! Five infielders including catchers were used. Catchers were required to repeat the coach's command on situation while making the proper throw to second, third and first. Not a few balls were either missed, or a guy, after making a great stop, followed with a bad throw. But it was fair. Only the best would be chosen. David Middleton and Carl Johnson drew praises. Ronald Gadsden and his twin brother Raymond would make the cut along with the veteran John Rivers and "Patchie" Gray.

Everybody could throw a baseball. Maybe it came naturally because every neighborhood had a house that was gutted and plaster provided the neighborhood kids with many "rock" wars. A nice fitting rock provided a lucky youngster with ammunition to throw at and kill birds. On creek beds, smooth stones flattened and formed by the pounding waves, provided a new avenue of throwing–skipping a rock across the water as far as it could go. Pitching then would not be a problem. Catching some of these pitchers might be.

Leroy Major was a big strapping twelve-year old and he could throw. Sidearm, submarine, with a touch of three quarter were his calling cards. The ball sailed in on a right hander and tailed out on a lefty. The danger of it all was that the ball was moving. There was no "window" to pick up where it left his hand. There were no speed guns in those days but to a man, we knew he was smoking that ball in the 70-80 range. Plus, he was so big that by the time he finished winding up, it seemed like he was in your face. He sure was in a batter's mind.

Then there were Allen Jackson and Vermont Brown. Allen, his long arms dangling, threw as hard as Leroy with a twist– he could throw a curve. Many an afternoon his father was a proud man as he signaled pitches to his son to throw and watched batters swing at the breeze with the strike three punctuation of the umpire. He was good and so was a kid called "Pop".

"Pop" pitched like Whitey Ford of the Yankees or more recently, Tom Glavine of the Mets. He could cut corners. In fact, Pop threw a cutter although I don't believe he knew it. The ball was not thrown really hard, but the cagey youngster had location. That location made him steady. A batter seldom received a walk. He had to earn his way on base and, for many, that was hard. Norman Robinson, Arthur Peoples and Roy Carter could catch Leroy, Allen and another strong pitcher, Admiral. That pretty much gave them an automatic shot at being picked.

Hitting for us was like dessert after a good meal. We played the field so we could hit. Sure, we had the usual batting practice type routine where a coach would throw "grapefruit" type pitches to a hitter who had fifteen swings. Many a ball was stung and many a player, who would later be cut, slept well that night. That day they hit like Willie McCovey or Josh Gibson. But the coaches had a surprise. There would be round-robin games to determine who could or could not hit. Of course, the pitchers were Allen, Leroy, "Pop", Admiral, Raymond, Maurice Singleton and myself. All were good.

This was show time and the crowd was large. Some sat in the stands; some loomed in the outfield and the baselines were dotted with people. Mothers, fathers, uncles, aunts, grandparents, school teachers–all were there pulling for "their boy". At the end of the day, everybody who knew anything about hitting could point to at least twenty or so youngsters that could flat out hit. Prime among these were Carl Johnson, John Bailey, Allen Jackson, Allen Mitchell, Norman Robinson and myself. We could hit. Now it was up to the coaches to decide whom they would pick.

"This was easy" says Mr. Dilligard, *"because we had teams already in place, so the managers knew the talent. We had a league. There they are. You saw them, now pick them. What happened was some new "ringers" showed up. Buck Godfrey, Bill's son, was a helluva athlete. He could play anything and hit like the devil. Then there was Clarence Admiral, a great pitcher. There was Major. Best pitcher I've ever seen. A big boy, too. Bailey could hit a ton and he was new. Mr. Burke had Allen Jackson, a switch hitter on lock."*

Allen supports Mr. Dilligard's contention.

"I was born on the East Side on America Skreet. When I was coming up, the East Side didn't have Little League. One day, my father brought me over on the West Side to swim. He always had a ball, a bat and a glove for me to play with. So I just started playing on Harmon Field.

"So one day, I was playing and Mr. Burke saw me and asked what team was I playing on? I say, 'What team you talking 'bout?'

"He say, 'You don't play no Little League ball?'

"I said, 'No, I live on Judith Street on the East Side.'

"He had never seen a little kid–my father was pitching–and he brought a bucket of balls and I was batting from the left and right (switch hitting). He ain't never seen a kid do that.

"And then one day, he wanted to see how I threw a ball. And he saw how I throw. He say, 'I ain't never seen a kid your age throw curves. Wait here 'til I come back' and (he) brought me a uniform. That's how I started playing Little League. Mr. Burke's team was the Police Athletic League (P.A.L.)."

In the final analysis, each coach was accorded 400 points to "purchase" a particular player. Mr. Burke had put a lock on Allen, but Mr. Singleton responded with a coup of his own by acquiring the rights to Leroy Major, destined to be the best pitcher in the League.

"I was the tallest boy out there trying out and they (the coaches) didn't want me to play. They say at my height, which was six feet, I couldn't be twelve years old. My mother gave them a call, and after they found out I was twelve, everybody wanted me on their team. But Mr. Singleton, the coach for Fielding's, he was determined he was gonna get me so I ended up on Fielding's team."

—Leroy Major

At the end of the draft, Major, John Mack, Arthur Peoples, John Bailey, David Middleton and Vermont Brown would play for Mr. Singleton and Fielding's. Mr. Burke's P.A.L. team boasted the acquisition of Norman Robinson, Carl Johnson, Maurice Singleton and Roy Carter, in addition to Allen Jackson. All of these guys became All Stars and I would have thought that at least two or three of these would be 100 point-players, but it was all in fun. Mr. Dilligard and Mr. Graham did a fine job, probably better than most because with younger and first year players, a coach had to work harder.

CHAPTER III

Purists say a four o'clock
And a morning glory are weeds.
Yet both open and close
At a designated time
And provide beauty and nectar
For the eye of the beholder
And the honey-bee,
All this without human care.
I guess we were the weeds.
We beautified the landscape
By adding rich, soft color.
We survived on little or nothing
Except mother's wit
And daddy's love
And we multiplied.

Before the first pitch was thrown, however, a few problems had to be addressed. Harmon Field was actually a playground and baseball/football fields. Smaller kids, older kids and adults all used the same field. Consequently, Little League games had to be completed in a timely fashion to allow the older crowd to play ball in the late evenings. Another problem was finances.

"We had little or no money and we needed things. Especially a portable fence. What we had to do, we finally got together—the men. We went to Sears and Roebuck and from our own pocket, we bought this folding, portable fence. It was four feet high by Little League regulations. Then we got some large containers, like big cans. Next, we got some cement and some stakes. We mixed the cement and poured some into each can. When the cement steeped, we put a stake in each one.

"When we played, we put the staked cans in designated parts of the outfield, again, consistent with the Little League distance rules. Now, we could put the fence up before games and take it down after so the bigger fellows could play. Everything about the field dimensionally was consistent with the National Little League rules. Rufus Dilligard took the responsibility of having the field "game ready". Mr. Burke would serve as umpire when he was needed. Allen Tibbs from the Y would bring a duffle bag full of bats over his shoulder to Harmon Field. He walked all the way because he had no car. He was very supportive and I appreciate that—we all did. Later, Bob Morrison, who owned a whole lot and had money, gave his financial support especially for the All Star trip. Everyone cooperated and everything went well."

—Lee Bennett, Coach

Opening day was filled with all the pomp and circumstance of a Burke High School graduation minus the controlled décor of this event. People were jubilant, boisterous, affable–this was their badge of accomplishment. A community had come together for their boys and they would make this day an event to be remembered for decades. Fathers greeted each other and a lot of hand shaking and backslapping took place. Mothers hugged each other and began a conversation that would end in sisterly fashion. Our coaches–Mr. Burke, Mr. Singleton, Mr. Graham, Mr. Dilligard and Mr. Bennett–beamed proudly. Relatives, friends, and curious onlookers greeted each other and actually took an interest in listening to one another's stories. No one sat in the smallish aluminum stands. Instead, everyone milled around engaged in some type of congratulatory talk.

Around 2:00 p.m., the coaches called for their teams to be properly introduced to the fans. They reacted with all the fervor they could muster. The aluminum bleachers was ill-equipped to hold the stacked, packed, excited crowd which eventually poured down each base path outside the chain-link fence.

When they had settled into an attitude of expectancy, each coach walked proudly to home plate, and introduced himself and his team members, name by name. The players, nattily dressed, lined up on the third base line and as his name was called, he strutted to home plate, tipped his hat to the crowd and walked down the first base line. Proudly, each youngster soaked in the sincere adulation of the adoring spectators. All of us felt special as we were individually and collectively cheered. Around 3:00, the umpire yelled, *"Play ball!"* The twelve or sixteen game season had begun. Fielding and Pan Hellenic took the field to warm up. This would be the first of many games decided by great pitching, outstanding defense and hard play.

The twelve game season progressed and, as expected, Mr. Singleton's Fielding's team took control. With Major and "Pop" mowing batters down, Bailey smashing homeruns, David, John and Arthur providing the rest, Mr. Singleton was all smiles, at least until Arthur Peoples pulled this stunt and realized that Mr. Singleton, like all the coaches, would discipline you.

"They always had a swimming pool behind Harmon Field. I'm givin' a point here. One day, we had a game and I went swimming. See, that was a No! No! I figured I'm gon' play anyhow. My coach, Mr. Singleton, found out and didn't start me. Little League only played six innings. He kept me on the bench 'til the final inning, then put me in the game.

"Ooooooooo! That hurt, but it taught me right then that you gon' go by the rules–don't care how good you are–you play by the rules or you not gon' play. You see that day, everyone was there. All your people, brothers in the stands looking for you to play and here you are on the bench. That hurt!"

Before long, Mr. Burke's Police Athletic team provided heat on the frontrunners. "Carlie" Johnson, their slick-fielding third baseman, was in a homerun contest with Allen Jackson, their top pitcher and centerfielder.

Norman Robinson was playing like Campanella and hitting like him. They had only lost one game. But before it was all said and done, Harleston and Pan Hellenic would make some noise.

Off the diamond Mrs. Bailey, Mrs. Dilligard, Mrs. Major, Mr. Jackson and others formed committees to raise money for balls, bats and gloves. Mrs. Dilligard started early by going into the stands with a plastic pail to ask for donations. Later, on Harmon Field proper down the right field line, supportive parents constructed a stand where they sold homemade pies, cakes, cookies and other pastries. Hot dogs, hamburgers, salt peanuts and soft drinks added to the list which spectators would purchase before and after games–never during games. Parents came to see their sons play ball.

At other times, Mrs. Bailey would organize teas and Mrs. Major would furnish a wide assortment of baked goods that she made from scratch. This was for adults only and none of us questioned this. After all, it helped us. Again, players and their parents would go on "caravan" picnics and fun trips to either Beaufort, Atlantic or McKenzie beaches. It was always Charleston hot so more time was spent in the water than on the beach.

To a man, the place we enjoyed the most was Daniels Island located across the Cooper River Bridge. The parents also liked it because, not only did they have fun playing softball, bid whist, checkers and bingo, their raffle of the $500 dollar money tree always brought in the most revenue. We liked it because it had canoeing. The canoe races—that was it! These were good days–good, clean days. Then the season grew interesting.

Harleston beat Fielding's. Brought on by Mr. Graham in relief with the bases loaded, I had struck out three straight batters, the last, John Mack. Boy, he raised Cain! A cocky fellow, he was totally embarrassed because he looked at the third strike, and the third strike was a fastball. That was unacceptable! A player was taught that if he must strike out, strike out swinging or if he must look at a called third strike, it had to be a breaking ball. To us, this was the Gospel. It never happened to John again. The next day, Clarence Admiral of Pan Hellenic three hit the P.A.L. No one, however, took a called third strike.

Things started to get exciting. Pan Hellenic with John Rivers hustling and the twins – Raymond and Ronald – made losses look good. Harleston beat P.A.L. and Allen Jackson to make some noise. But in the end, it came down to talent and to a lesser degree, coaching.

Fielding's just had too many players. Police Athletic League had almost enough players. John Bailey and Leroy Major slugged the ball like Willie Mays and Orlando Cepeda for Mr. Singleton. Carl "Carlie" Johnson and Allen Jackson did the same for Mr. Burke. In the end however, the pitching of Vermont Brown and Leroy Major was the deciding factor. Fielding's, P.A.L., Harleston and Pan Hellenic – that was the pecking order or finish of the 1955 season and this was expected. Then came the big reward, the selection of the 1955 Charleston Little League All Stars. Each player knew that this was big. The team selected would go national.

"Understand now, we had a good season and played strictly by the rules of the National Federation. In 1954, we played among ourselves. Pan Hellenic played an 'all star' team which consisted of players from the other three teams. The next year (1955) would be different because we had decided to go to the Nationals in Williamsport, Pennsylvania. We had prepared our teams for fierce competition. We placed them in a confidence that bordered on cockiness. We knew we could whip everything in South Carolina. So we–myself, Walter Burke, Lee Bennett, Archie Graham, Ben Singleton, along with the president of the Y, Bob Morrison–began the selection process. We voted on the boys' ability, attitude, versatility and team loyalty. When we finished, I thought we had the best of the best."

—Rufus Dilligard

Anticipation, replaced by reality, followed by jubilation was the mood as the coaches voted, then read the names. Except for the absence of Clarence Admiral, Rufus Dilligard Jr. and Allen Mitchell, the selection was fair. Fielding placed six players on the team: John Bailey, Vermont Brown, Leroy Major, David Middleton, Arthur Peoples and John Mack. P.A.L. followed with five: Allen Jackson, Norman Robinson, Maurice Singleton, Carl

Johnson and Leroy Carter. Pan Hellenic placed Charles Bradley, John Rivers and George Gregory. Harleston finished with two – Vernon Gray and myself. Unbeknown to these youngsters, they would add a very unique chapter to African-American history.

The Team

John Bailey – first year player whose greatest asset was his ability to hit the long ball. Cool-headed and deadly in critical situations. Played a sound left field. Total team player. *"I was picked because I was a good hitter. I batted clean up on my team. I was also picked because I was a team player."*

Vermont "Pop" Brown – the lefty with the cutter. A student of pitching, he could throw it all. His curve ball seldom hit the sweet spot of a batter. His asset was the ability to pitch on the corner. Had excellent control. A batter had to hit to get on base. An adequate first baseman and hitter. At his absolute best in top games. *"I knew I could pitch. In fact, I was good at it. When time came for Mr. Singleton, my coach, and the other coaches to pick the All Star team, I knew I would be chosen."*

John Mack – cocky infielder with a knack for big plays. Nothing passed him at third or shortstop. A wiry fellow who had a great arm. Loved competition and attention. Was solid hitter who seldom struck out. *"I could play any position. I knew I would be chosen."*

Vernon Gray – an infielder who became an All Star through hustle. Could play all infield positions. Great base runner who put pressure on pitchers. A solid hitter with a good feel for the game. *"When time came for the coaches to choose the All Star team, I was nervous. I made it because of hustle."*

Leroy Major – would have made the majors as a pitcher. At a strapping six feet, and side arm or three quarter delivery, he could bring it. Jammed right handers; broke the bats of left handers. His submarine pitch was just unhittable. He had three pitches: fast, fast, fast. The problem was they came from all angles. A humble team player. *"I had a fast ball and since I was tall, it really was fast. So I became the star pitcher and was picked for the All Star team."*

David Middleton – One of the best hitters ever. Relaxed at the plate, he could spray the ball to all fields. Focused and deftly slick second baseman. Never made mental errors. *"I could field and I could hit. I knew I would be an All Star."*

Arthur Peoples – my catcher. Always dusty from hustle. Lack of size made up in energy and guts. Could throw and hit with consistency. Caught "Pop" and Major. Controlled the infield and gave his pitchers the edge by calling a good game and executing his position. *"I was picked to be an All Star through hard work and dedication to the game."*

John Rivers – second year shortstop who seldom made errors. Leader of the team either by sound or action. Always on top of the game. A natural leadoff hitter who sprayed the ball around. Always a factor in the overall game. *"The coaches chose the best players from the four teams. These guys became the Charleston Little League All Stars. And I was one of them."*

Charles Bradley – energy and hustle were his calling cards as an infielder. Smallish guy who played big. Guts and heart. Another spray hitter who made things happen especially under pressure. Excellent on hit and run. *"I was a team player and could play any position."*

Norman Robinson – would have made majors as catcher. Knew the strength and weaknesses of every hitter. Always made the right call behind the plate. Had an arm like a rifle. Line drive hitter who hit for average and power. Mentally tough and emotionally ready for all games. *"I knew I could catch and hit. I made the team because I knew how to set up batters by calling a good game behind the plate."*

Carl Johnson – the best third baseman and best hitter on a team of great hitters. Had range, arm and intelligence at "hot corner". Perhaps, never made an error. Could hit for distance or average. Whatever the situation, "Carlie" was ready. He would have made the majors. *"I was the best third baseman in the league. In fact, I was the only third baseman picked. I wasn't surprised to be picked as an All Star."*

Maurice Singleton – could pitch a fastball with the best of them. Coach's son who became a student of the game. Situational ballplayer with a cool steadiness. A decent bat. Great one-two combo with Jackson as pitchers for Mr. Burke's P.A.L. team. *"I could pitch and run, but I was picked because I played smart."*

Leroy Carter – great arm, solid hitter who could run. Good centerfielder with range. Always kept teammates loose with jokes, chatter and hustle. *"I was good and played for Mr. Burke."*

George Gregory – Pan Hellenic's steadying force. A study in quiet confidence. As catcher, solidified the infield. Caught Clarence Admiral, one of the best pitchers who did not make the All Star team. A steady hitter with a good arm. Extremely coachable. *"I out-worked a lot of players and kept a good attitude."*

Buck Godfrey – great arm, great bat, great speed. First year player. Pitched, played centerfield and third base for Harleston. Long ball hitter who could hit for average. Known for hard-nosed play and hustle. Described by many as Westside's best player. *"My team always came first so I played hard and aggressive in every situation. This attitude of do or die and the ability to hit, pitch and play centerfield got me selected as an All Star."*

Allen Jackson – would have made the majors. Gangly with long arms, he was perhaps the best all round player on the team; could hit for power–led Little League in homeruns or average. Arm like a rocket either from centerfield or the mound. As a pitcher, had a great fastball made more menacing by his repertoire of curves and a change up. The complete package. *"I could pitch, hit and field. I knew I would make the team. When* *time came to pick the All Stars, I knew I would be one. The best players were picked by the coaches and I was good. I think the team was a team of superstars. I don't think no team could have beaten us. Like me, Major, Buck–we were fantastic as far as strong arms and control in pitching. I don't think nobody could hit us. And plus, I was the homerun leader that year. But Major, Buck, Carlie, Norman, Bailey—all of them could put it out–along with the rest of the fellas. The teams we would play would have no impact on us, no chance."*

REQUIEM – NO EULOGY

Perhaps they will come forward
Now that he is dead.
The New Orleans Picayune

The "gentleman" mentioned in the following chapter as the one responsible for stopping the 1955 Little League tournament was just a product of the times. After all, one cannot expect a John Brown in a state that just recently (2007) resolved its Confederate flag dilemma and still has not developed educational acumen comparable to the national level. One must also understand that to be locked in a historical situation based upon primitivism, classism and racism cannot permit other than distorted and deceptive thinking. In a system where any injustice can be justified by reference to a social study, a biblical allusion or political euphemisms, one expects to find at the very core of its foundation, the vitriolic propaganda and perpetual brainwashing of African-American people who represent so much power and whose united potential is so great, they must be stifled.

These same people, because they are living symbols of the hypocrisy of the Bible-toting southerner, become a more abstract, sometimes visceral aberration of hate gone wild. Their presence is a constant reminder of the southerner's inability to accept his wrongdoings and get right with the Creator. True to form, those that have a conscience and are embarrassed by what they have done, distill the seat of conscience with bourbon and continue their satanic fears borne by hate, fear and cowardice. In the end, the one who victimizes becomes the victim and the targeted victim becomes the victor. It implodes because lies cause moral rot which festers like a pus-filled sore only to swell and burst and stink. The stench causes outrage because there are only two medical examiners who perform the autopsy: the enlightened youth and the mocking finger of the real history.

The reason is a simple one. Hate begotten of hate is by hate destroyed. The energy required for this perpetuity implodes. Only a cinder is left. The victor, on the other hand, eventually realizes that to be the object of this fusillade of insanity, he must be more powerful, more menacing, more beautiful and more intelligent than he had ever imagined. In the duress of pain, he has learned love for his family, his people and himself. In the fullest magnitude of triumph, blinders cast aside, he has learned forgiveness. He, alone now, stands at the fore, strong and complete.

The question is then put: How does a man, so limited by his history, gain a place of responsibility? Isn't it a fact that men like these are dangerous? Ignorant, they play on the fears of the equally ignorant who follow blindly like hounds in a fox chase. Again, the answer is simple. They accomplished some physical feat (that no one else would try) consistent with the doings of warmonger Presidents, who despite their ineptitude for adjudication, annihilated the Native People and bestialized the African. In a word, they became local heroes, national heroes. And they were dubbed to have the foresight to lead and maintain oppression.

But give the southern "gentleman" his due. At least, he was cognizant of the great players of the Major Leagues, Negro Leagues and the Navy in World War II. No fool he! In the same light, give our coaches and parents the credit they deserve for being sophisticated enough to understand the positive ramifications of our oral history. In doing so, they prevented their innocent twelve-year-olds from becoming strange fruit hanging from the tree of hopelessness. They did not negate our history. Our heroes looked like us and probably saved our lives.

CHAPTER IV

The Trip

Gray sky lined Arctic white;
There lies a solar contest.
Blue sky, lined death pink-
An orange, red wafer
Scowling in the West,
Cold weather ahead.
Snow capped waves,
A greenish, brown sea-
Wind strong, blustery-
Whipping from the East.
Storm on the way.

We were just eleven and twelve-year-old little boys who played baseball. We knew nothing of life beyond our neighborhoods and Harmon Field. Boys our age from forty-eight states were looking forward to playing for a National Baseball championship in Williamsport, Pennsylvania. Not one of us in the summer of 1955 doubted that we would whip everyone in our home state of South Carolina at Greenville then move to the regionals in Rome, Georgia to continue our quest. It would not happen.

During the season, "scouts" had come to our games. Some of us thought they were from the majors. Of course, with this revelation, we played even harder. The "scouts" continued their presence taking notes and pointing at certain players and quietly whispering to one another. The southern "gentleman" came on more than one occasion. While attending a game between Fielding's and the P.A.L., he was shocked when he overheard Mr. Singleton say aloud that we would have an All Star team with the intention of playing in the South Carolina Little League tournament. To our dismay, the "scouts" were not from the Dodgers or Braves. They were "runners" from the North Charleston parks and recreation superintendent, the southern "gentleman".

"I heard rumors, but I never saw Danny Jones at Harmon Field. Other whites came and they could have scouted us, but I didn't care. They knew we were good; they knew we were good. Somebody must have seen us. I know the worst thing that could have happened to them was to play us and get whipped. They probably did not want to risk that. White fellas used to be at practices and games and that All Star team was a bunch no one could take lightly. So it wouldn't surprise me that word got back to top level whites that we were good, too good."

—Rufus Dilligard, Coach

A staunch segregationist, this "gentleman" led the boycott which eliminated the city of Charleston Little League tournament. "Races shouldn't mix" was his rationale. Undaunted, our coaches continued our July practice for the state tournament in Greenville, South Carolina, by playing real games against the '54 All Stars. Not to be outdone, the southern "gentleman" played on the ignorance and fears of the politicians and their followers so vociferously that sixty-one teams pulled out of the competition to protest the entry of the all-black Charleston Little League All Stars a.k.a. Cannon Street Y.M.C.A. All Stars. The state tournament canceled, we became the unofficial South Carolina State Little League Champions. It had a good ring to us for this reason. We all bolstered ourselves with the only idea we could fathom. Those teams were afraid of us.

"(Strangely enough), I didn't realize (the truth of this) until someone told me Mr. Danny Jones, the man who kept us from playing, was all ready to have the white teams play. But, he came to (Harmon Field on more than three occasions) to scout us. I guess he saw, at that time, that we were good as or better than rumor had it. He probably realized that we would have beaten the white team who would represent them. So they weren't going to allow that to happen, especially in the second year of integration. (Brown vs. the Topeka, Kansas Board of Education officially integrated schools in 1954.) So that's why they canceled the contest."

—Leroy Major

Our coaches explained that we could still play in the regionals to be held in Rome, Georgia. Eight state champions would compete there and we were the champions of South Carolina. In the first week of August, 1955, the Rome Little League delegation sent a regrettable letter to Peter McGovern, Little League President, informing him that because our team had won by forfeit, we could not participate. We were hurt, confused. In the end, it looked like we would never play.

The good-doing people of Williamsport must have felt our pain. As a gesture of good faith we were invited to Williamsport.

"The Williamsport people invited the boys up at their expense because they couldn't play the white boys in Charleston, South Carolina or in any place in the South. But Bob Morrison took care of expenses not covered by Williamsport. The coaches went with the understanding that the Charleston All Stars would not play."

—Walter Burke, Coach

Mr. McGovern took initiative. He understood the idea of Little League. In fact, when the southern "gentleman" proposed two Little League championships – one segregated, of course, Mr. McGovern responded aptly: *"(The Charleston youngsters) became innocent victims of alien influences that have deprived them of beneficial associations and opportunity to meet and know other boys in Little League Baseball."* This statement spoke volumes of the integrity of Little League Inc.

Anyway, someone cared other than our parents, coaches and good-doing adults. In a small way, we all felt that we whipped the southern "gentleman" and his race-baiting cohorts. We little boys had even beaten the Klu Klux Klan who, some say, had staged the largest cross burning rally ever at the news of our "championship". With a mountain of youthful exuberance and a sliver of hope, we still believed we would play. But, we would have to pay our way. Our parents, our coaches, our churches, our businesses, our adult supporters, our neighborhoods came together in a common effort. They would help in sending us to Williamsport and hopefully we might play the remaining twenty-eight teams there. We still had a chance.

The trip would soon begin. We would travel the 748 miles to Pennsylvania on a yellow school bus owned by Mr. Esau Jenkins. On board, would be fourteen team members and four coaches: Mr. Ben Singleton, Mr. Lee Bennett, Mr. A.O. Graham and Mr. Walter Burke (Mr. Dilligard's wife Catherine had taken ill so he did not make the trip.) The Y.M.C.A. was represented by Mr. R. Penn, secretary, and Mr. Bob Morrison, president. As it turned out, the bus was ill-suited for such a long trip. There was no air conditioning, no soft cushioned seats, no road ready power train. We had fun and we sure had drama.

For most of us this was our first trip away from our families. Mothers, fathers and friends cried openly as we began boarding the "big yellow". John Bailey's mother, eyes brimming with tears touched me when she hugged him and said, *"John, here's twenty dollars. Put it inside your belt until you get to Williamsport. Be careful, call me and, most of all, be sure to say your prayers tonight."* Our mothers were held in the highest esteem so this was a tender moment, many of which took place that afternoon.

The coaches packed four ice cold watermelons, chipped ice in a foot tub, lemonade and sodas of all flavors. In addition, there was a two gallon jar of pickled pigs' feet, a super sized bread pudding, mounds of Charleston style crispy fried chicken and all the candy a player could eat. Twenty sheets and pillow cases along with seventeen large fluffy pillows completed the travel fare. As expected, we ate from the time we left Charleston to about ten miles from Williamsport.

Charleston cheered as we pulled off. We were proud and excited little fellows. What we did not realize was that we were trail blazers, writing a chapter in American history. We were just ready to get to Williamsport and play baseball. There were new uniforms to be worn, new gloves to be broken in, new hats to shape and new Louisville Sluggers to launch homeruns. We played cards, bingo and other games. Some of the players had small radios that they put to their ear to listen to music. We played with and talked to each other. We played tricks on each other. We joked about Vernon's first pair of pajamas. We laughed at Pop's big first base glove his father had bought. We slept. We had great fun.

About twenty minutes later, 1955 America showed its face. Just outside of South Carolina, we stopped at a restaurant. A tall, drunken white man who stood outside yelled, *"Niggers, get out of here now! This restaurant don't serve niggers!"* Immediately, Mr. Burke, who was a Charleston policeman, came to our aid. After conferring with this man and his buddies, Mr. Burke signaled for us to get off the bus. Some of the players and coaches went in and were served. The white men sped off into the night.

In Virginia, we were stopped by a state trooper. We discovered later that he wanted to know why the big yellow bus was loaded with luggage and Negroes. Again, Mr. Burke handled the situation. One player said that during the conversation, Mr. Burke flashed his badge. That must have been the solution because soon after, we were allowed to continue our journey. What else could happen? Oh, the bus.

Across the state line of Pennsylvania, the bus sputtered to a complete stop. The driver jumped out along with Mr. Singleton and Mr. Bennett. We could hear talking, and soon banging and clicking sounds resonated from under the hood. Soon the driver returned to his post. From outside, there was a yell: *"Crank it! Crank it!"* The motor coughed, then came alive with a steady drone peculiar to a school bus. Mr. Singleton and Mr. Bennett stepped back on the bus to the sound of our whistles and cheers. We moved on to the highway. It was early morning.

About five to ten miles from Williamsport, a smell like burnt plastic hit our nostrils and smoke billowed from under the hood. We were in trouble again. The bus had caught fire. The South Williamsport Fire Department came and the cause became clear. In the hurried effort to fix the motor, our driver had left the emergency brakes on. Soon after their help and once again in shape, "big yellow", with its cargo of Charleston's best, cruised into Williamsport, Pennsylvania.

The coaches and Y.M.C.A. officials met with some smiling organizers. They acted like they were glad to see Mr. Singleton and the others. Our skepticism relaxed. Not long afterward, we followed a car to Lycoming College, and we were given rooms. This was actually happening for us. We cleaned up, and Mr. Singleton and Mr. Burke called us to their room. Much to our surprise, we were given new white caps and brand-new white T-shirts with "Cannon Street All-Stars" emblazoned on the front. Everyone was smiling.

Next we ate breakfast in the dining hall with the other teams. For the first time in our short lives, we did not feel the tension of being an all-black team. Some teams were integrated. Others had guys who looked like us but spoke Spanish. We thought to ourselves, the North was different. Black, white, and all others all ate together.

Finally we marched in with the other teams on to Stotz Field. We had never seen anything like it—grass on the infield and a short fence. Boy! This was our day. We knew it when later in left field, we experienced a kind of celebrity.

Allen Jackson picked up a misplayed ball by the leftfielder of a team warming up and fired a strike to the catcher. Phew! That did it. He was an instant cult hero because I don't believe anyone there had seen an arm with that type of velocity and accuracy. The rest of us followed along. After all, we must be awful good to be teammates of Allen.

People brought food to us as we sat in the stands. We signed autographs. We absorbed it all. This feeling of elation had replaced all the doubts. We felt like All Stars, like champions. Incredulously, as we enjoyed our star status, our coaches and Mr. Morrison were negotiating with Mr. McGovern and his staff to allow us to play at least one game. But the Little League was not persuaded and we were finally told the gut-wrenching truth on the bus ride back to Lycoming College. We were not going to play. There was no immediate response, only death-watch silence. We had been on an emotional roller coaster for too many days. Finally, Allen Jackson vented. This doleful outburst spoke for us all. *"We had come all the way up North for nuthin!"*

After a mostly sleepless night, we again washed, put on our street clothes and tried to eat without success. We boarded the bus which took us to the ballpark, the velvet grass, the short fence, then we took our places in the stands. Before very long, the public address system announced us by name before one of the games. Reluctantly, the fourteen of us stood. Then something happened that was surreal. Some one person shouted, *"Let them play! Let them play!"* Like a chorus on cue from some unseen hand, everyone in the stadium took up the chant: *"Let them play! Let them play! Let them play!"* They meant it. They knew we could play. To these people, in that moment, at that time, we were not a black team. They saw kids, just like their own. Their view was that of a level playing field. We hugged each other; the coaches hugged each other; Mr. Morrison and Mr. Penn hugged each other. These people gave us credibility, credence, love. We had the endorsement that we had needed. No, we did not play; however, we won and we would go on winning, but with a great price. Something ominous, painful, exasperating had taken place that day. Its effect was felt the next day and years to follow.

CHAPTER V

The dynamics of living-
The perforated shield of deception-
The moulage of rhetoric-
The predilection for deceit-
The asymmetrical convolution of lies-
The aborted attempt
To control the diameter
Of our being
So Powers and Principalities
Could control
The circumference of our essence.
The contortion of truth-
The pissoir of morality-
The panacea of "dry-bone" religion.
As relegated by King James
And his scholars
Minus William Shakespeare
Who wrote <u>Othello</u>
And catapulted the careers
Of Ira Aldridge and Paul Robeson.
The fanfaronade of history-
The Native People,
The Seminole and Chiricahua-
They saw.
Geronimo was a shaman.
The Middle Passage-
Nat read; Toussaint read;
Vesey read; Prosser read.
They had knowledge
Honed by the blue steel

Shaft of wisdom
And they instilled fear.
Toussaint, Garvey
Dubois and Malcolm-
Education and economic independence-
This commands respect,
Strikes doubt in the mind of the adversary.
He reassesses his strategy
But comes to a painful realization.
The very system he designed to destroy
Actually served to create
The real men.
This is what the manchild discovered
This is the manchild's rite of passage
Into manhood.

The next morning, as we boarded the bus, which would transport us home, we took a final gaze at the Susquehanna and the adjoining misty hills and mountains of western Pennsylvania. This pastoral setting of calm and serenity seemed unaware of the plight of the members of the Charleston Little League All Stars. Each of us knew something bad had happened. No one spoke. No one looked at another. Nods and grunts communicated all. The adulation and fanfare of yesterday were replaced by the depression and dejection of today. We could not leave Williamsport fast enough.

As we took our seats, the prevailing mood can best be described as the atmosphere of a wake with the accompanying emptiness one feels in the pit of the stomach after viewing the remains of someone real close. No kind words, no soothing touch, no powerful medicine could give relief. Appetite wanes and fists clench. Anger, confusion and frustrations hold dominion. Each player is alone, fighting his own demon. Collectively, the enemy is too many, too powerful, too sophisticated. We had been robbed and were impotent to do anything to the perpetrator. He had committed the crime and escaped into history with impunity. Our words were stifled by the shyness of youth.

What we could not fathom or swallow as youngsters, we comprehended and digested fifty years later as adults. In Williamsport, reality-steel hard and ice cold—had smacked us in the face. We were changed forever. Broken forever was the halo of innocence that had steaded us all our lives. Its loss opened the floodgates of cold knowledge, cynical and brutal. Because of this, a little boy became a manchild and never again would he surrender his complete trust to any adult. Skepticism bordering on cynicism now stood at the fore. The blister of not playing became a sore. The sore became a hardened callous. The callous became the manchild, and this is what he learned.

"When we were on our way to Williamsport, I was happy. That didn't last long once we got there. We found out we weren't going to play. I was especially down hearted when the people in the stands started to chant: "Let them play! Let them play! Let them play!" After that, I looked at things the way any little kid would–depressed, can't play, long trip, for what? If we could have played, we would have been recognized and some of our dreams (would have come) true."

—Allen Jackson

"(The Williamsport experience for me was bitter-sweet.) Believe it or not, I just felt the impact the other day. A little boy from Williamsport, Pennsylvania, wrote a letter to me. And (as) I was reading the letter to my wife,...the tears (started) and just kept rolling down (my face) and I couldn't stop them from rolling down. It was then I realized that those adults stole the dreams of little boys...and I said (that) I hope that doesn't happen to other kids. But it's still happenin' because kids don't run the world, adults do. If the adults didn't stop us, we probably would have played.....

"You see I was slated to pitch the very first game and not only do I think I would have done a magnificent job, but all my teammates would have done the same, especially playing against another race. I think we all would have been a little hyped. Remember, we had magnificent players because from the four teams we had, they (Mr. Burke, Mr. Dilliard, Mr. Bennett, Mr. Singleton, and Mr. Graham) picked the best players for the All Star team. With this team, no one would come close to beating us."

—Leroy Major

"Now you never know until you face something, how you'll react. As a group, we felt that we were the best team to represent Charleston, South Carolina, in the World Series. We went to Williamsport, Pennsylvania, and in our minds, we was gonna play. Before the games started, we were informed that we wasn't gon' play.

"That was a shock. We feel that we came all the way to Williamsport, Pennsylvania and didn't participate. Truthfully, I figured we had the best team and that hurts. When you're young kids–11-and 12-year-olds–you feel like a small portion of a big process. Everybody else was playing the game that we love and we couldn't participate.

"I was bitter at the time and sometimes I'm still bitter because the people never could seen us play (never got a chance to see us play) all because my skin is different from your skin, but we all speak the same language and (bleed the same color blood). Some of the white kids up deh (Williamsport) want us to play anyway. But the politics of opinion won out and young people suffer."

—Arthur Peoples

"We were planning to go to Williamsport and there was no doubt in my mind that we were gonna play. I subsequently learned that our managers and Mr. Morrison thought that if we could get there, we would play.

"Well, we made it there. We stayed in the same college dormitory; we ate in the same dining room; we did everything but play. That was a disappointment because then I realized we were here but were not going to play. Of course, I thought that they didn't want to play us because they were afraid of us. I thought they were afraid we would whip them, beat them. Are we that good? Were they (that) afraid of us? It was kind of convoluted, but that's the way I saw it. We will never know. But what if?"

—John Rivers

"As I look back and think about the Williamsport thing, I realize the coldness of the people (of no color). That was a hurtin' feelin' not to be able to play in the Little League World Series. I mean you jus' sittin' there watching

everybody else play. The only thing left to us was to discuss among ourselves what we (possibly) could have done (if we were allowed to play). The field–beautiful field; the fence–the fence was short (the distance needed to hit a homerun).

"This shocked me. During that time, I didn't realize they had darker guys there. We thought they were black. In fact, they were black but they came from the Dominican Republic or Puerto Rico and spoke Spanish. To their advantage, they were not American. To our disadvantage, we were American. But we were black, like them, and spoke English. So we were in the stands. It was hurtin; really hurtin, but we made the best of it. We enjoyed the trip to Williamsport. I think that was the best part of the bad experience. But I never played baseball again, not even in high school."

—Carl Johnson

"I mean all I could see came from the perspective of a twelve-year-old kid. I was hurt; we weren't going to play. I learned later that we won the State Championship by default and that the teams we should have played refused to play us. Consequently, we were "awarded" the State Championship by default. For a while, that consoled me, but I felt that deep hurt, every time I saw baseball. Every time I saw Little League, I used to turn (the television or radio) off. I mean about twenty years ago when the series was televised, I tried to look but I revisited that anger. Rather than do that, I turned the television off.

"There is no question in my mind about how we would do. There were five of us who looked at the field at Williamsport. It seemed shorter, seemed smaller. We had played under wretched, hard conditions at times. Our field was not pristine. The outfield grass wasn't cut. (We had no infield grass.) The game could be played on a fast field or slow field. We adjusted. But we could hit the hell out of a baseball. Like I said, there were five of us that could hit a homerun at will–myself, Buck, Major, Carlie and Allen. So offensively, we felt we could beat the pants off any team.

"We had great pitching with Pop, Allen, Leroy Major–I mean these guys could throw curves at twelve-years-old which is just phenomenal. And so we had talent and good coaching. (Mr. Burke, Mr. Dilligard, Mr. Singleton, Mr.

Bennett and Mr. Graham taught fundamentals and game strategy like professionals. And they could not be intimidated. This was important.)"

—John Bailey

Since we were baseball players and good ones, this manhood should have begun at Martin Park. Martin Park was the big time and our only alternative. After Pony League, there was no Colt League. If we wanted to go to the big league, the Pony League at Martin Park was our next step. However, the psychological and emotional trauma of the Williamsport experience would translate into many of the All Stars' decisions to play or not to play Pony League baseball at Martin Park. A few of us would play the full three years; others would play two years; still others would play one year and call it quits. Sadly, the majority would not play at all.

"The next step for us was Martin Park. It was different. When I left Little League, I went into a situation where the guys were older and more competitive. They had better skills. I only played there two years and it was different. I guess I became interested in other things then. I didn't have the same fire I had in Little League. Something just left me. After that great disappointment, I just didn't have it anymore."

—John Bailey

"After Little League, I played two years with the Pony League at Martin Park. Martin Park was a large ball field where they had a gas station 'cross the street behind the left field wall. Once you hit a homerun and it landed in the gas station, you were big time. You were a hero. These were good days. If you could play at Martin Park, you were good."

—Allen Jackson

"From Little League I went to Martin Park, the Pony League which was a real difference experience. Over there was the best of the best from the Eastside

and the Westside. We had one fellow we used to call 'Con'. He was the only pitcher I had ever seen who could pitch a game while everybody but the catcher sat down on the ground, and nobody could hit him. Another difference is that we had signs in Little League, but when you move up to Pony League, there were a lot more signs coming from coaches on the base paths.

"Martin Park looked more like a baseball field 'cause they had a fence. When you hit your homerun, you really enjoyed it when you see it going over the fence rather than the Sears & Roebuck fence we had in Little League that we had to put up before the game and take down after the game. Martin Park had stationary fences. But only the best played."

—Leroy Major

"So much for that. After Little League, the better players went to the other league (the Pony League at Martin Park). For some of us that would be our high school since Burke had no baseball team. The best of the West Side and the best of the East Side played at Martin Park. The East Side had formed a Little League franchise in '55. Again, I played well enough to earn a spot on the Blues. I only played two years and actually never played baseball again."

—John Rivers

"Beyond Little League, I played one year (of baseball). At Martin Park in the Pony League, it was different. You see when you move up a level, another level, now you have to bring your game up another level. The first year up there, you realize whether you could cut it or not. I realize my game wasn't as mature as the boys at Martin Park. I was on a team, but I even forgot what team I was on. That's how long ago it was and how tough it was."

—Arthur Peoples

"When I used to come across the Cooper from Riverside Beach, I would see games being played at Martin Park. I knew I wanted to play there one day. In

fact, all of the fellows on our Kracke Court Sluggers team wanted to play except three. Mr. Lawrence Johnson talked to my parents about playing for his team the Hawks. That was all I needed to hear. For the next three years, I would be playing for the Hawks and Mr. Lawrence at Martin Park."

—Buck Godfrey

CHAPTER VI

Martin Park

"Con" could throw a baseball
Through a concrete wall
If anyone got a foul tip
When batting against him,
He had a good day.
Only Boy Blue could hit "Con".

I have no idea when Martin Park became the site of the Charleston Pony League. I do know this. If there was a weakness in one's game or his confidence level was shaky, it was to his benefit that he stay home. There were no scrubs here. A ball player was expected to have game because he competed at the highest level every instant at Martin Park.

For many of us, this was the first time we played in a closed park. Martin Park was enclosed by a chain link fence. There was grass on the infield; however, what fascinated us the most was the prospect of putting one out of the park over the left field fence and see the ball bounce into the ESSO station across Cooper Street. For those of us who succeeded, it was the best, most thrilling feeling in the world. And instantly, everyone saw a player differently. He was a celebrity, a hero. He had hit a ball over 320 feet and he was either fourteen or fifteen years old.

The names of the coaches were many, as the transition period from '55, '56 and '57 would indicate. They were at a given year: "Hoggie", "Ben", "Okra", Mr. Lawrence, "Lucky Lou", Fred Ballard, Peter Mazyck or Mr. Lemon. All these men cut their baseball teeth on the East Side. They were well-respected, tough-minded "headers" from the largely secretive, sometimes violent world of Charleston's waterfront. Except for Mr. Lawrence, who worked at the cigar factory, they knew the hardness of working in the bowels of ships depending solely on his "breasted" or his "gang". Physical strength used wisely was respected. Wisdom made one see; instinct guided the responses. Most of all, however, they knew the game of baseball.

If memory serves me well, Mr. Ballard and Mr. Lemon coached the Bears. Peter Mazyck and "Hoggie" coached D.P.O. Ben coached the Blues. "Okra" coached the Pirates and Mr. Lawrence and "Lucky Lou" coached the Hawks. When the Hawks were not playing, "Lucky" served as umpire.

The year I came, 1956, the Pirates had a pitcher named Donald Morrison, nicknamed "Con". He had long arms and a long lean body that gave leverage to a fastball that could puncture a steel wall and a curve that "dropped off a table". What hurt the hitter was a windup that was smooth and structured to impact its fullest power at the peak of delivery. What confounded the hitter's dilemma was the aforementioned curve, which came from three angles with the change-up as his best pitch. Leroy Major, who played for the Bears, probably describes Con's presence and "Okra's" philosophy best.

"'Con'" and I started for our respective teams that day. I believe they were the home team. I was a rookie, but I struck out the side in the first inning. Then the Pirates took the field with 'Con' throwing BB's to his catcher. Now this is the stuff of legend. 'Okra' told all of his players to sit down at their positions – except the catcher, of course. Well, 'Con' struck out the side on nine straight pitches. Ramsey, my teammate, bunted for a single and I hit a knuckler off the end of the bat for another hit. The funny thing is the umpire, 'Lucky Lou' was ducking

most of the game. He didn't know or care whether it was a ball or strike. 'Con'
fanned nineteen."

—Leroy Major

To keep Martin Park at the top of baseball's elite was no small chore. Coaches worked at it. These men would scout players from the West Side at Harmon Field and the East Side in the Borough. The East Side had applied for and received a Little League charter in 1956. Naturally, a rivalry started between the two sides of town. It came to a fruitition when the first All Star series began in that same year. The winner of the best three out of five games was the champion.

The West Side would play two games in the Borough then the East Side would play two games at Harmon Field. The deciding game, if the series went to five, would be played at the field of whoever was the home team that year. According to Mr. Bennett, this was great for communities. Fathers bet; fathers would brag on his son or sons; fathers would sometimes cause confusion. Mothers were just proud of their boys and came to see them play. The players themselves took it all in stride. Most of them knew each other either personally, from attending school or church with each other, or by reputation. They respected each other and some would become teammates at Martin Park. After all, Martin Park was the Pony League and featured the best of the best. The Pony League coaches loved the All Star games. It showed them the product they needed to win. The Bears and the Blues had pretty much cleaned house up to 1956. The Hawks with Mr. Lawrence at the helm won in '57 and '58 all through the "draft".

The Hawks drafted young in '56. From the East Side Mr. Lawrence picked up Eggie, Boy Blue, Bobby Seales, Fred Smalls and Frank Green. From the West Side he picked up myself. The following year, Mr. Lawrence added Michael Green, Frank's brother, from the East Side and from the West Side Raleigh LaRoche, Raymond and Ronald Gadsden, Frank and Stevie Hamilton, Clinton Dilligard and Frank Godfrey, my brother. The Hawks became an instant contender because they were strong up the middle with Eggie at catcher, Seales at second, Fred Smalls at short and myself in center.

For whatever reason, most players at Martin Park came from the East Side. Kids from Anson Borough Homes, Wragg Borough and the area from Columbus Street to Calhoun Street and rectangled by King and East Bay Street dotted the Pony League rosters. Kids from the West Side were noticeable primarily by observing those who were not there. The ones who came made their mark. In addition to those already mentioned, there were Alvin Thompson and Clarence Admiral, both great pitchers, and five players from the '55 Williamsport All Star team.

Perhaps Martin Park was closer geographically to the East Side. Perhaps since all of the coaches had East Side roots, kids from the West Side did not come. Perhaps there was the competition. Maybe some could not play there. Perhaps some parents and kids had a real or imagined fear of the East Side "reputation" for whatever. No doubt there were some characters like "Black", who could make a West Side kid feel miserable just by being in the area. But "Black" was cool. Like many of us, he loved to fight and would fight and we developed a friendship based on that premise. However, the game was the thing. Everyone came to see good baseball and "Black" was just one of the fans.

The Blues with Allen and Harold Jackson, Leroy Major and John Rivers were the favorites, especially because of their winning reputations and Ben, their coach. "Con" had turned sixteen so "Okra" Crosby's Pirates would be competitive but not formidable as in the past. D.P.O. was D.P.O. However, everybody knew the team to watch was the Hawks. And they delivered.

In pivotal games of the fourth week, Boy Blue of the Hawks beat the Blues although Allen and Leroy sent a missile a piece to the ESSO station behind left field. On Wednesday, Buck blanked the Pirates on a three hitter 7 to 0. Michael Green and Bobby Seales shut out D.P.O. as the Hawks pounded out sixteen hits–twelve for extra bases. At the midway mark, the Hawks were the frontrunners sporting a hefty 12-2 mark, a position they never relinquished.

Similar to Little League, something important was being discussed in a hushed manner. It was All Star games time and people were excited. The managers huddled and met late into the night. It was discovered that the talk concerned our opponent, Acabee Pantry. They would play us–not as an All Star team, but as Acabee Pantry. We knew they were good. All the teams from Union Heights were good. This team, however, was so special that the managers of the other teams in their league conceded to Acabee. Acabee would be their All Star Team.

A lot was on the line. The managers at Martin Park knew it. The team was chosen. Peter Mazyck and Ben would manage. The site was Strawberry, South Carolina. I was to pitch the front end of the doubleheader. Admiral would pitch the second game. In the heat that Saturday, we were soundly whipped in a doubleheader: 14-4 and 7-2. Then something crazy happened.

CHAPTER VII

Smooth as butter
And sharp as Masie's straight razor,
He rose to the top
By his own volition.

Slam! *"Ten to one, my team, the Hawks, will beat your team next Saturday 3:00 at Martin Park!"*

This was my coach, Mr. Lawrence, talking. He had his index finger planted on a hundred dollar bill. I had never seen a "Benjamin" in my life.

"Bet!" the manager from Acabee Pantry countered as he laid a ten spot on the table. *"We'll be there."* Gyp, the trusty hustler, picked the bills up and placed them with a wad of money he had in a leather bag.

Now one must understand. Acabee Pantry had just whipped our Martin Park Pony League All Star team in a doubleheader and Acabee Pantry, at that time, had a winning streak that extended back about three or four years. They were from Union Heights known for cutting, fighting, generally raising hell and baseball. I don't know if they followed an age limit, but they sure enough followed a "best" limit. Man, could they play! But Mr. Lawrence had made his bet in front of everybody. Knowing how he operated, he had seen something. Acabee Pantry had a weakness. More importantly, my coach was embarrassed for Martin Park baseball on that hot day in Strawberry, South Carolina. At the least, he wanted payback.

As I was about to get on the bus headed back to Charleston, Mr. Lawrence pulled me aside. He whispered, *"Meet me at the park tomorrow at 2:00. You gonna pitch against them boys."* Before I could respond, he was gone. I had just walked the first six batters I faced and had hit the seventh. I told Eggie and Seales. They smiled the gunfighter's smile and exhausted, fell asleep.

When Mr. Lawrence showed on Sunday, I was ready. He had brand new balls, a facemask and a catcher's mitt. We met at home plate. He began by telling me the importance of the game. He told me that Martin Park's reputation was on the line. (I knew it.) He also told me that there would be a big crowd there. All the people from the Borough, Mexico, North Charleston, the West Side and the East Side would be there. Then he said, *"I'm going to prepare you myself. We are going to add a sidearm curve as a change-up and perfect the forkball. We also will use the fastball on the corners. After you warm up, I want you to throw fifty pitches at three-quarter speed and we'll be done."*

For three straight days, I followed the schedule outlined by Mr. Lawrence. Then on Wednesday he revealed the real plan. He brought "Lucky Lou", his assistant coach, to serve as umpire. What Mr. Lawrence had done was genius. He had written in his notes the uniform numbers of the players from Acabee Pantry. By each he had their batting strengths and weaknesses. Terms like "long stride", "foot in the bucket", "strictly pull", "uppercut", "open-stance", "closed-stance" were used. My knowledge of batters, I found, was contingent upon these designations. Pitches thrown to right locations would be the strategy for winning.

I pitched a full seven inning simulated game at nine pitches an inning–sixty-three pitches in all, with the intensity of a real game. "Lucky Lou" simulated a real umpire. Always on point, Mr. Lawrence had given this information to Eggie, the Hawks catcher. Also, he practiced our team at night. On Thursday and Friday I was told to just ice my arm and rest. I didn't ask any questions.

Saturday came bright and sunny. The sky was Columbia blue. I walked the three or so miles 'cross town to Martin Park. From the bottom where the swings and sliding boards were, I saw four red and gray uniforms. When I reached first base, I was greeted by Seales, Eggie, Fred Smalls and Boy Blue. Blue had assumed his favorite position under the bench in the shade, half asleep.

It was 1:30 p.m. Mr. Lawrence and "Lucky Lou" came at 1:45. Acabee Pantry–three van loads of coaches and players—rolled up at the same time. The crowd started to pour in from the Cooper River Bridge side. Aiken and Hanover Street produced a steady line of people from everywhere–old, young, dead–they were there.

The umpire leaned against the stands on the Acabee side. At 2:30, they took the field for warm-up. Mr. Lawrence had me on the pitcher's mound down the first base line. I warmed up for fifteen minutes. My arm never felt so strong. Mr. Lawrence took the mitt from his hand and held his red, swollen palm to me. He simply said, *"You ready, let's go."*

The Hawks took the field at 2:45. Boy Blue was the only change. He played first base instead of right field. Eggie, Ronald Gadsden, Fred and Seales completed the infield. My brother Frank, Michael Green and his brother Frank completed the outfield. I had never seen them look that sharp. Everything was moving like clockwork. *"Play ball!"* That was it. Martin Park's best against Acabee Pantry.

Mr. Lawrence was giving the signs to Eggie from the bench. First pitch, change up curve–strike one! Second pitch, forkball–it broke and dropped left of the leadoff hitter. Third pitch high inside heat. He swung but never saw the ball. Strike three! The second and third spot hitters went the same way. We ran to the bench.

Acabee threw their ace. He was a southpaw and he did not pitch in the All Star game last week. Fred Smalls led off with a walk and stole second on the first pitch. Bobby Seales laced a double on the third pitch. Eggie ripped the first pitch for a triple. The place was going wild. Mr. Lawrence flashed the suicide squeeze sign on the second pitch. I was at bat. The second pitch was a hard slider. Eggie was almost home and I just managed to bunt the ball down the line at third, but I was thrown out by their third baseman. Boy Blue worked the count to three and one and hit a ball to right center that people still talk about. It one bounced to the fence approximately 400 plus feet away, good for an inside the park homerun. Our next two hitters flied out. Hawks 4, Acabee 0.

The game rolled along as Mr. Lawrence had planned. On the way to striking out fifteen of the twenty-two batters I faced, we managed to only give up one run. In the fifth, Fred made an error at short. Right then, I wanted to do something to Fred. The next hitter hit a lazy fly that turned into a double. No-hitter and shut out–gone! After that, clockwork. One, two, three. The final score: 7 to 1. Eggie, Seales, Boy Blue and Ronald had three hits a piece. I didn't manage one but somehow it didn't seem to matter.

When their last batter fanned on pure white heat, the place went wild. Back slapping, hand wringing, cartwheels, the split. Gyp was collecting money. Everybody was happy. They had participated in history. The fifteen of us had gathered at the mound to watch. We shook hands with each other and hugged, but this was more of a respect thing for each other's game rather than an effort at "showboating."

Mr. Lawrence was beaming. He was proud. He fumbling said, *"Thank you, boys. Now go and shake Acabee's hand."* We did and that was cool. There were some old dudes on that team, but we had gained their respect. We had already respected them. As Mr. Lawrence told us after the crowd had left, *"In order to whip someone as we whipped this team today, study them, always respect them, but never fear them."*

"Did we represent well enough to regain our respect?" I asked

He retorted with a question, *"Ain't we the Hawks and ain't this Martin Park?"*

We all smiled. Lots of pressure was released by that win. "Con" had done his part and so did many others to make Martin Park's reputation as the program for the best solidified. The Hawks had added an exclamation point. My father bought me a link sausage with mustard and a Nehi grape soda. I knew then that we were bona fide. My Daddy didn't give anything to anyone, unless he had earned it.

CHAPTER VIII – EPILOGUE

Song For My Father

My shoes would be shined
And the house would be warm
A long time before I awoke.
I could vaguely remember
A rough face implanting an equally
Rough kiss on my forehead.
Then the door would open and close,
And he was gone for the day.

> *He was seldom at home*
> *But his presence was felt.*

Sometimes when he returned from work
He'd be so hot
That his supper was watermelon,
And I'd listen to him
Slurp up the pink juices.
He would pat me on the head and smile,
Then he'd bathe, go outside on the glider,
And fall asleep.

> *He was a man*
> *When it was hard to be a "boy."*

At other times, he would come home
And change into the white coat.
That meant he was serving a party.
I would strain to wait up for him

And sometimes I would succeed.
But he never knew.
All I wanted to do was make sure
That he was home.

> *He led by example*
> *Because he was quiet.*

On work Saturdays we'd simonize cars
At five dollars a whop
My arms would be tired
And I wanted to quit,
But I never could
Because I would see him
Lick sweat and keep on rubbing
'Til the finish shone like glass.

> *He led by example*
> *Because he was quiet.*

On other Saturdays
We'd crab or go to the beach.
He couldn't swim then
And he still can't,
But he loved the water
And he was there,
And that was all that mattered.

> *He was a good father*
> *When others had quit.*

When John Holmes and Rubenstein
Or Mose and George Frost
Would come around,
I'd get mad
Because I knew they'd be chasing
Red-Eye,
And Red-Eye would win every time.
It lay Daddy down
And made him snore
And he was cranky on Sunday.

> *A working man must have his day,*
> *Then pay the price the morning after.*

On the following Monday
He'd sit in the big brown chair,
Read the paper and bite his thumb
And he'd look at his boys
And tease his wife
Then he'd switch on the radio
To the country music station
And fall fast asleep.

He was a father who bit his thumb
And thought about his stouthearted boys
Who knew nothing of life.

On Friday nights
After the Dupont came,
Mr. Macbeth would come up
And we'd all watch
The Friday night fights.
And Daddy and Mr. Macbeth
Would punch themselves into fatigue.

He always said that Joe Louis
Could whip Muhammad Ali.

Then one day the Revolution came –
And Daddy wanted to kick
Bull Connor's butt
And punch George Wallace
Back into the last century.
Instead, he joined hands with King
And protested peacefully
And won anyhow.

He led by example
Because he was quiet.

He glowed when I received
A scholarship to Delaware.
His face shone
When Frank made a 4.00 at St. Aug.
He smiled when John graduated
From Hampton and the James.
He peacocked when Hunts finished
SMU Law School.

He finished the eighth grade
But he's the smartest man I know
Because his degree came
From the University of Life
And he led by example
Because he was quiet.

Now he visits Miss Nellie
And the cats on the corner
After fixing breakfast for Mama
And manicuring the churchyard.
So I guess one can say
He's unselfish and kind
At least around Kracke street
Where everyone smiles
When they see Mr. Bill.
I have always realized
How lucky I am
And how fortunate my children are
Just for my being able to say:

"Hello, Mr Bill." And he replies:
"Whadya say, boy?"

The strength of a real man is judged by his ability to succeed under overwhelming odds or survive under oppressive circumstances. If he buckles under the pressure, he is considered a loser and consigned to the graveyard of failure and the resulting inferiority. In the course of *The Team Nobody Would Play,* I have spoken about the trinity of man – that is father, husband and man. This becomes a special situation when dealing with the African-American man. Demasculated and mentally raped, he had had to fight a lonely battle of worth. He's had to bargain for his manhood in a struggle that could end in death. He's had to protect an exploited woman and maintain his sanity, because many times, she could not understand that he, too, was a victim of exploitation. Finally, he had to be the model, a figure of strength to his fruit, who many times, could not understand his fatigue or temper or gentleness. A paradox one says. Yet, this is my father and many black fathers, myself and my teammates included.

In our story, in our time, men—our fathers, our coaches—are synonymous with unselfishness, sacrifice, humility, wisdom, strength, love, support, courage, discipline, direction, organization and integrity. As a result, we, as ballplayers of this association, had a heads up on what it took to be a man, a father. This association made us grow.

We learned about fatherhood and sacrifice up close and personal. Despite the late hours spent in coaching us, which sometimes caused "unkind" words from his wife, Pan Hellenic's Mr. Bennett raised four girls, a boy and a grandchild, all of whom received college degrees. Despite working in a segregated civil service system, he was promoted from classified laborer to second-class supervisor. This is a testimony to his resiliency and courage.

"I have no regrets," he says, *"because the boys who went to Williamsport and the boys who did not make the 1955 All Star team are doing well. In spite of all that we experienced, they became successful—teachers, architects, principals, private business. The Bible says, 'If you cast your bread upon the water, it'll come back to you.' When my boys came home, they come to see me and I feel good. I was glad I was able to be a part of this, and if I had the chance to do it again, I'd do it all over!"*

Similarly, it is no small wonder that Leroy Major had a problem refusing his children. *"What I've gotten from my dad, it's hard for me to refuse my kids because when I went home and told my dad I needed a baseball glove, he said, 'Let's go!' He never said, 'Wait a minute!' He always took me to get (whatever). In anything, he supported me. He never discouraged me and I let my kids know this. Whenever they ask for something, it's hard for me to say no because I reflect back on my dad. I just know what he would do."*

Again, like many of our fathers, including the "loud talking" Mr. Johnson, Carlie's father, Allen Jackson's father never missed a game, and he unselfishly found time to help Leroy Major develop as a pitcher, treating him as he would his own son. As Allen fondly remembers: *"My father and my mother would not miss a game. They came to cheer me on. When I played the outfield, my father would use hand signals to put me in the right spot especially when Buck or Major came to the plate. More than once, it was the exact spot they hit the ball...So that was nice.*" Support and encouragement was always there.

My daddy, like Allen's, always came to see me play. From Little League to Delaware State, he was there for his boy. I learned many things from the man. He supported his family by working three, sometimes four jobs; he always found time for the four of us–all boys–either by taking us crabbing, swimming or simply picking up dinner and riding out to watch the trains go by. More than anything, I noticed how he treated my mother whom he lovingly called his "brown bomber." Total respect was given to her from the time she arose to the aroma of strong coffee and fried bacon until she went to bed with him huddling then cuddling closely. Because of this, I always had a deep respect for women.

Not unexpectedly, all of us have become great fathers. I talk about how proud I am of my two children, Colin and Rashan; John Rivers boasts about his daughter, son and three grandchildren; Carlie wears his grandson's high school cap. His grandson, who is a great football player in Jersey, is his grandfather's pride and joy. To a man, all of the guys have taken fatherhood seriously because we had great mentors.

Doing a job well, no matter how insignificant or unimportant it may seem to others, was also essential to our growth into manhood, because it kept us humble and developed a strong sense of teamwork. A poignant example is the work of Mr. Rufus Dilligard.

Everyone knew that Mr. Dilligard alone prepared the field for play. This was his baby and no one challenged this. He took immense pride in this endeavor. "*When we started our twelve game schedule, I was in charge of the field. I remember the fence that was paid for out of our pockets. It had to be set up and taken down after each game. But when it rained, by George, I caught the devil.*

"*I would put a fifty-five gallon drum in the trunk of my car and fill it with dirt. I wanted to see the boys play so bad. Sometimes, it took three, four or five trips. I would dump the dirt at the muddiest spots, clean it, rake it and get the field ready. Believe me, I had it squared for game time. Some people frowned upon this work as dirty."* To us, Mr. Dilligard was a man who didn't mind getting a little dirty because his job may have been the most important of all, and we appreciated it.

John Bailey gives us another take on teamwork. *"Since I'm in the Building Construction field, team is critical. I assemble my team every morning–the plumbers, the bricklayers, the carpenters, and the laborers. I give them an exact plan to follow. In this aspect, teamwork learned in the Little League helps tremendously. An example is having the insight to see where guys sometimes need a little encouragement on a daily basis. One may have had an argument with his wife; another may have had too much to drink that weekend. In the end, it is important to explain to the workers that in order to get from point A to point B, we got to have togetherness, teamwork. That's the only way we can accomplish this and Little League baseball taught me this."*

Leroy Major gives teamwork a much more profound application associating it with building character. *"Teamwork teaches a person to treat everyone with respect. Again, I tell my children (that) the same way you treat the President, treat that drunk on the corner...If Jesus came back as a drunk, are you gonna miss heaven? If Jesus came back as Danny Jones, the man who kept us from playin, will I miss heaven? No! So you respect all people. I'm not gon' take time to hate Danny Jones or anyone else. I never heard my parents speak about the other race in a negative way. I try to teach my children the same."*

Discipline was psychological and subtle. Other than Arthur Peoples' swimming blunder, this embarrassing situation happened. A player may find his name scratched from the lineup. Downhearted, he took his place on a "special" part of the bench where there lay an envelope with his grades inside. One of the coaches had been alerted by the teacher or parent, or the coach had gone to school himself. Poor grades or, God forbid, poor behavior could set one up to be "traded." Just kidding. But "just passing" was not tolerated.

As a life lesson was taught, discipline became life lessons. In this case, the game was football and it concerned me, Buck Godfrey. Late in a

Homecoming game, I intercepted a pass and returned it 68 yards for a touchdown. We won 6-0. Never one for seeking praise, I slipped out of the locker room and headed home. At the door, I was met by my mother performing like a cheerleader and reciting the cheerleader chants. Then she started hugging me and kissing me. My father, seated in his chair near the stove, never moved or looked at me. When my mother left the room, he finally responded. He stood straight up, walked over to me, looked me straight in the eyes and matter-of-factly uttered these words which stung me and froze me in time. *"You shoulda scored. You eat a damn nuff."* And he left the room for bed, just like that. He had always taught me to be thankful for any success and fly the middle course.

Later that night, as I lay awake listening to night sounds, he stole into the room as I pretended to sleep. He leaned over my brothers, planted a hard kiss on my forehead and said earnestly, *"Billy, I am so proud of you."* Then he was gone. I smiled, snuggled under the covers, and slept the most restful sleep of my young life.

With the nurturing we had, many of us have accomplished some outstanding feats. They are listed below with no names affixed:

- On-site architect for the Martin Luther King Center for Social Change in Atlanta, Georgia and King's burial crypt.

- Omega Psi Phi Fraternity's National Scholar of year in 1965 graduating with a 3.61 G.P.A.

- On-site architect for the Columbus, Georgia, School for the Performing Arts.

- Founder, President and CEO of a $20,000,000 construction firm.

- Responsible for the management, rehabilitation and health care of 5,500 inmates before retiring.

- Won a football championship with an all black team in Georgia's highest classification (AAAA) in 1995. The first African-American to do so.

- Formed a mentor-student program to aid in academics in the Low-Country.

- Established the Worthington Valley Dolphins, the first predominantly black team in DeKalb County, Georgia.

- Hit .511 to win the Central Intercollegiate Athletic Association batting title in 1965.

- Owner of business responsible for the detailing of over 1,000 cars, trucks and SUVs.

- 217 of his football players have received full athletic scholarships.

Indeed, we have been truly blessed because of our nurturing environment.

Our coaches were remarkable men. Unselfish and humble to a fault, they gave us life's intangibles. We won with humility and lost with dignity. We competed with every fiber of our being, knowing that if we did all we could do, if we left it on the field, we had no regrets. We learned respect for our teammates, our opponents, ourselves. The reader will notice that in most cases, we called our coaches "Mister." This was the way he carried himself—confident, focused, manly.

They were always neat. Mr. Dilligard and Mr. Bennett worked at the Naval Shipyard. Mr. Burke was a Charleston policeman. Mr. Singleton was a custodian. Mr. Ballard worked the waterfront. Mr. Lawrence worked at the cigar factory. Mr. Graham was a cab driver. We never knew it. At games or practice, they wore clean shirts and pants. They were gentleman first, and with all the coaching and tension, we never heard a cuss word, not one.

Finally, they knew the game and they taught us well. Fundamentals, fundamentals, fundamentals. It became a habit. They were also fearless. At the time they coached, the challenges they presented to southern America is the stuff of legend. I believe we followed their lead because of who we are. Thanks to these men will never be adequate enough. We have to live like they did and give. This was their legacy and this is what we must do.

Again, when true reflection is completed, when true insights are disclosed, we come to this realization. Our neighborhoods were ours and they were unique. Each had its own rhythm of life. Carlie had to literally exorcise demons to get to practice; Bailey could only play outside at a certain time in Strawberry Lane; Major and his family would sleep at night with the doors unlocked.

Each neighborhood in our story gave these life lessons freely. It taught love, responsibility, and discipline. It taught pride, survival, and respect. A child respected his elders, his parents, women, himself. Yes, sir; thank you, ma'am; Mr. or Mrs. so and so; may I and please; all of these came naturally. Swearing or pouting was taboo. One took his life and his behind in his hands if he did either.

Parents were many and watchful. The teacher, the coach, widows, spinsters, the barber, the mailman, the good time woman and the bootlegger, the policeman, even the undertaker could, by a word or gesture, make for a day to rejoice or a night to regret. These observances would be relayed to a biological father and mother who lived at a place called home. In the end, they exacted punishment or gave rewards. They provided stability. In this regard, we were extremely fortunate. The village helped in rearing us but most importantly, the persons that we saw everyday were our role models. And they lived in the house with us. Life was truly good.

These same people–Mama and Daddy–greeted us and consoled us upon our return from Williamsport. Emotionally and psychologically, we were scarred. Our chance to play and win a Little League championship for the city of Charleston and the state of South Carolina was gone forever. More importantly, our love for the game remained, but our desire to compete waned. For more than a few of us, that was the last attempt at organized competition. Other than Allen, Arthur, Major, John Rivers and myself, I don't know who else competed at Martin Park and beyond.

Just suppose we were afforded the opportunity to play in a Pony League of our choice and move on to the Colt League. Just suppose we were born above the Mason-Dixon line or in Canada where the playing field might be level. Just suppose we could speak Spanish and came from Puerto Rico or the Dominican Republic. Just suppose we were born and reared any place where we would never feel the tension of being black and good. Just suppose.

Our heroes had a plan though. They had seen many things and experienced more. There were opportunities still available to us. To a family, no parents mired themselves in self-pity. They never allowed us to dwell on what might have been. Instead, they chose for us to run the course. As my Daddy use to say, "This too shall pass," and it did. Their directive was simple and firm. Finish school and get to the business of living. Learn from the past, but live in the present. The future is no guarantee unless wise investments are placed in the present. We learned these lessons well and followed suit. But in a quiet moment, alone and pensive, we replay the events of half a century ago, because in the final analysis we played the game of baseball so well that no one would play us. So forever we will respectfully and affectionately be known nationally and locally as <u>The Team Nobody Would Play</u>.

The Lineup 2008

School Teachers: Leroy Major
                                              Buck Godfrey

Architects: John Bailey
                                              John Rivers
                                            Norman Robinson

Industrial Cleaning Business: Arthur Peoples

Car Detailing Business: Carl Johnson

Corrections Officer: Allen Jackson

Lockheed Aircraft: Vermont Brown

Chef: Vernon Gray

Painting Contractor: David Middleton

Limousine Service: Maurice Singleton

Home Bound: John Mack

Deceased: Charles Bradley
                                            Leroy Carter
                                            George Gregory
                                            Walter Burke
                                            Ben Singleton
                                            Rufus Dilligard